MW00957615

Montana's CAST-S

Crisis Action School Toolkit on Suicide

2017

This Montana CAST-S Toolkit was developed by co-authors Dr. Scott Poland and Dr. Donna Poland in collaboration with Montana OPI, SAM, DPHHS, Big Sky AACAP, and NAMI Montana for the express use by Montana schools. Other agencies or individuals wishing to use materials must obtain permission from the authors by contacting spoland@nova.edu.

Published November 2017

Editorial and layout support was provided by
Peter Christensen, Punchline Communications Inc.

About the Authors

Scott Poland, EdD

Currently a professor at Nova Southeastern University's College of Psychology, Dr. Scott Poland is also the co- director of the NSU Office of Suicide and Violence Prevention in Fort Lauderdale, Florida. He has worked in schools as a psychologist or a director for twenty-six years and is still very involved in school crisis response and consultation. He has recently provided on-site assistance after suicides in several school districts. As survivors of the suicide of his father, he and his family are examples of those who never believed a suicide could happen.

After being promoted to director of psychological services in Cypress-Fairbanks ISD and facing the suicides of several students, Dr. Poland became dedicated to suicide prevention. In 1982, the district superintendent asked him what he was going to do about these suicides. At the time, he answered that he did not know. Figuring out how to prevent youth suicide has been his highest professional priority ever since, and he has presented more than 1,000 times on the topics of school crisis and suicide intervention.

Dr. Poland is a licensed psychologist and an internationally recognized expert on youth suicide and school crisis, and he has authored or coauthored five books on the subject. Additionally, with his wife, Donna, he has authored the Suicide Safer Schools Plan for the state of Texas. Dr. Poland is a past president of the National Association of School Psychologists and a past director of the Prevention Division of the American Association of Suicidology. He has testified about the mental health needs of children before the U.S. Congress on four occasions and has personally assisted school communities after sixteen school shootings and after acts of terrorism, natural disasters, and numerous suicide clusters.

Donna Poland, PhD

Dr. Donna Poland has been a professional educator for thirty-seven years, of which twenty-seven years were in public schools in the great state of Texas where, she says, "everything is BIG!" She remembers her surprise, as a first-year teacher, when she discovered that her middle school classes averaged over thirty students, and she had six classes each day! She very quickly discovered that she needed to get to know her students and build a respectful and nurturing environment before she could even consider teaching the curriculum. Having that vital connection with each student was the reason she walked joyfully into the building every day.

After seventeen years in the classroom, Dr. Poland began her administrative journey as a director of instruction, an at-risk coordinator, an associate principal, and, finally, a principal. Immediately upon taking a leadership role, she was faced with the tragedy of a scholar athlete taking his life by suicide just days before he was due to enter ninth grade. Tragically, that was not the only suicide she experienced. Every year resulted in working with parents, staff, and children in the aftermath of a death by suicide or an accidental death. The next ten years (at a small private college-preparatory school in Florida), Dr. Poland continued to need her skills for developing programs, educating staff, and working with parents regarding the signs of depression and suicide. After experiencing a death by suicide, especially of a young person, she says one never forgets the details of a life ended too soon and the haunting questions of "What did I not see?" and "What could I have done?" Dr. Poland hopes the information contained in this toolkit will help you in your work with young people.

Acknowledgements

The following individuals were interviewed and generously provided input on the development of CAST-S:

Karl Rosston, Suicide Prevention Coordinator, Montana DPHHS

Edith McClafferty, Montana Senator

Kirk Miller, Executive Director, School Administrators of Montana

Matt Kuntz, Executive Director, NAMI Montana

Tiffany Hanson, Treasurer, NAMI Montana

Dr. Keith Foster, Medical Director of Psychiatry, Shodair Children's Hospital

Dr. Heather Zaluski, Shodair Children's Hospital

Dr. Len Lantz, Big Sky Psychiatry

Steve Thennis, Principal, Helena High School

Administrator Health Education Division, Montana Office of Public Instruction

Coordinated School Health Unit Director, Montana Office of Public Instruction

School Mental Health Coordinator, Montana Office of Public Instruction

Coordinator Project Aware, Montana Office of Public Instruction

We Would Like to Hear from You

We encourage schools that are using or have used the CAST-S to update us on their stories and successes.

Please send your stories to either of the following:

NAMI Montana: Matt Kuntz, matt@namimt.org

Montana Suicide Prevention Coordinator: Karl Rosston, krosston@mt.gov

Big Sky Chapter of AACAP: Len Lantz, bigskyaacap@gmail.com

We Would Like to Hear from You

Table of Contents

Tools for Schools and Appendices

INTRODUCTION

Introduction

Why We Have the CAST-S

In 2017, the Montana state legislature passed House Bill 381, which addressed suicide prevention in schools. In addition to reiterating the prevention-training recommendations for school employees outlined in the 2015 legislation, the 2017 legislation required school district trustees to establish policies, procedures, or plans related to suicide prevention and response. Crisis Action School Toolkit on Suicide (CAST-S) is designed to assist school personnel in Montana to implement the required legislation and is not intended to be a substitute for training. The Tools section of the CAST-S outlines recommendations for training and crisis-action protocols for responding to suicidal students, notifying their parents, documenting all actions, and recommending needed supervision and services for the suicidal students.

The Importance of Crisis-Response Protocols

Crisis response protocols are essential when students are detected as suicidal to provide a standardized response to safeguard students and protect schools from liability. School personnel in Montana must be knowledgeable and passionate about the need for suicide prevention in schools and recognize that the basics of suicide prevention are the same regardless of school size.

Crisis response protocols can ensure the following:

- Immediate response
- Accurate assessment of community resources
- Suicide rate reduction
- Standardized approach that follows best practices
- No need to create proper responses in the heat of a crisis and in a potentially counterproductive manner
- Legal/litigation risk reduction
- Responsiveness to community needs
- Screening for depression, the biggest risk factor for suicide
- Support for other efforts/training on suicide prevention for children in the community

The Unique Needs of Montana for Suicide Awareness, Prevention, Intervention, and Postvention in Schools

Youth suicide is a significant problem in Montana where a community- and state-wide emphasis on prevention is needed. Montana faces many challenges due to its diversity, the isolation of many small communities, and the lack of mental health services in parts of the state. **It is essential that these challenges not stop a single school from developing suicide-prevention, -intervention, and - postvention plans.** Schools play a critical role in suicide prevention for current students and for future generations of Montanans, who need to know more about the warning signs of suicide and how to take action to save a life. In 2015, the governor of Montana signed House Bill 374 requiring the Office of Public Instruction (OPI) to provide guidance, technical assistance, and training materials to schools on youth suicide awareness and prevention. House Bill 374 also encouraged school district employees who work directly with students to complete at least two hours of training on youth suicide awareness and prevention every five years.

The state of Montana released the *2016 Suicide Mortality Review Team Report* (MSMRT) based on a review of 555 suicides that occurred in Montana between January 1, 2014, and March 1, 2016. The report has many important implications for the prevention of youth suicides. Unfortunately, Montana consistently ranks in the top five of our nation's states having the most significant problems with suicide. The report identified 27 youth suicides for youth between the ages of 11 and 17 during the period from January 1, 2014, to March 1, 2016. The majority (81%) of the youth suicide victims were male, and 19% were female. 78% of the suicide victims were Caucasian. 63% of the youth suicides involved a firearm, which is above the national average of 39% in the same age group.

The *2017 Montana Strategic Suicide Prevention Plan* states that suicide is the second leading cause of death for children and adolescents in Montana and highlights many prevention efforts across the state, which include working collaboratively with stakeholders, agencies, and schools. The plan identifies a number of challenges for suicide prevention as it is a frontier state with many isolated communities and, unfortunately, a culture of acceptance of suicide. Stigma about receiving mental health treatment also exists, as do concerns about maintaining confidentiality about receiving treatment in small communities. There is a shortage of mental health treatment facilities, especially for inpatient treatment, and a shortage of psychiatrists. Firearms are readily available in most homes, and there is a problem with underage drinking. The report also identifies the need for culture- and tradition-specific suicide- prevention information for American Indians, and OPI has developed culture-sensitive forms for suicide assessment.

The MSMRT includes the *2015 Youth Risk Behavior Surveillance Survey* (YRBS) for high school students in the state of Montana. The chart below compares Montana high school students with the nationwide survey.

2015 YRBS Survey Statement	High School Students:		7th- and 8th-Grade Students:	
	US Data	Montana Data	US Data	Montana Data
...felt sad and hopeless for two or more weeks in a row in the past 12 months.	28.3%	29.3%	N/A	26.1%
...seriously considered attempting suicide during the past 12 months.	17.7%	18.8%	N/A	17.1%
...made a plan about how they would attempt suicide during the past 12 months.	14.6%	15.5%	N/A	14.2%
...attempted suicide during the past 12 months.	8.6%	8.9%	N/A	11.6%

The MSMRT also includes data from the Montana Youth Risk Behavior Surveillance Survey for seventh- and eighth-grade students with regards to depression and suicide plans and actions. Unfortunately, there is no data to compare the survey results for Montanan middle school students with their peers nationwide. **It is important to note that new YRBS data is available every two years, and schools can access their own local data at OPI.**

Special recognition should be given to the leadership that is evident in the recommendations made in Montana's *2016 Suicide Mortality Review Team Report*. The report stresses the importance of universal depression screening in schools for 12- to 17-year-olds and the importance of best-practice suicide assessment. Included in this toolkit (Tools 14A and 14B) are examples of a suicide risk assessment: the Columbia-Suicide Severity Rating Scale (both a brief and a long form).

The MSMRT also stresses the importance of safety planning and recommends that Montana Medicaid write a policy that requires the use of safety planning with any patient who is positively screened for depression. Tool 17 provides a sample safety-planning form. Three of the top six recommendations from the report concern children, including the use of early elementary interventions such as the PAX Good Behavior Game and the Good Behavior Game. Additionally, the MSMRT recommends standards for safe storage of firearm in homes.

Native American Youths

Native American youths have a significantly higher rate of suicide than any other ethnic or racial group of youths in the country. Montana's Department of Public Health & Human Services (DPHHS) has an excellent report entitled *Montana Native Youth Suicide Reduction: Strategic Plan, January 2017* on their website (dphhs.mt.gov). The CAST-S will need to be adapted with cultural sensitivity for each tribe in future projects that include meeting with tribal leaders to get their input about how best to proceed to prevent suicides of American Indian youths.

> **Facts on the tribes and their reservations, economy, and tribal councils can be found on their websites.**

Blackfeet Tribe of the Blackfeet Reservation

Chippewa Cree Tribe of the Rocky Boy 's Reservation

Confederated Salish & Kootenai Tribes of the Flathead Reservation

Crow Tribe of the Crow Reservation

Fort Belknap Gros Ventre and Assiniboine Tribes of the Fort Belknap Reservation

Fort Peck Assiniboine and Sioux Tribes of the Fort Peck Reservation

Little Shell Chippewa Tribe (state-recognized)

Northern Cheyenne Tribe of the Northern Cheyenne Reservation

How to Use the CAST-S

Background

In the following sections of the Montana Crisis Action School Toolkit on Suicide, the authors Dr. Scott Poland and Dr. Donna Poland have worked collaboratively with the Montana Office of Public Instruction (OPI), the School Administrators of Montana (SAM), the National Alliance on Mental Illness (NAMI) Montana, and Big Sky Regional Council of Child & Adolescent Psychiatry (Big Sky AACAP), who are eager to assist Montana schools and to know how the implementation of the CAST-S progresses. We encourage schools who use CAST-S to update us on their stories and successes. Please find contact information in the front matter of the toolkit. We have reviewed the materials on the OPI website (opi.mt.gov/Programs/HealthTopics/SuicideAware.html) to provide guidance, technical assistance, and training materials to schools on youth suicide awareness and prevention. We also reviewed the suicide prevention information on the Montana Department of Public Health and Human Services (DPHHS) website (dphhs.mt.gov/amdd/suicide), including the 2017 Montana Strategic Suicide Prevention Plan and the 2017 Montana Native Youth Suicide Reduction Strategic Plan.

It was our goal to tailor the CAST-S to the unique needs of the Montana schools, and towards that end we have interviewed many key personnel in NAMI, OPI, DPHHS, and SAM. We recognize that Montana has 496 school districts, which vary considerably in size and available mental health resources. The CAST-S emphasizes the need for a school or district to have personnel who are specialists in suicide intervention. These are most likely school counselors; however, in the smaller districts and in isolated schools, this role may need to be filled by a trained administrator or even a lead teacher. This person would be the key educator asking a student direct questions about suicidal thoughts and suicide plans, and he or she would provide the needed supervision and parent notification and work towards securing mental health services for the student. Although the tasks above may sound daunting, the action protocols in the CAST-S outline all the steps, and the Columbia-Suicide Severity Rating Scale (C-SSRS) can be used by anyone. The most isolated schools in Montana will be the most challenged to obtain mental health treatment outside of the school for a suicidal student, but treatment facilities must be located even if they are a significant distance from the school. We have provided Tools 31 and 32 to help school personnel identify and work with mental health services in their community or region before and after the suicide crisis.

The CAST-S will build on the outstanding momentum for suicide prevention already in place in the state and on further collaboration among all stakeholders in Montana. School administrators are the key to increased suicide-prevention efforts in the state, so the CAST-S is designed to provide them with best practices and to encourage school districts to form a task force on suicide prevention and partner with local community and state resources. The toolkit provides a District Action Steps Chart (Tool 1), which outlines key leadership steps for school administrators to implement a comprehensive suicide-prevention/-intervention and postvention program in their schools. We recognize the opportunity that schools have to prevent youth suicide, and we believe it is their ethical responsibility to do so, and that positive educational outcomes are founded on mental health and a sense of belonging. It is our hope that, as a result of increased suicide-prevention efforts in the Montana schools, future generations will gain knowledge that will dispel myths about suicide, provide suicide-prevention resources, and empower everyone to take actions to prevent suicide.

Many Montanans know someone who died by suicide. The term "died by" is much more acceptable to survivors than the word "committed" as it takes the emphasis away from it sounding like a criminal act. It is our hope that educators in Montana will remember to use the term "died by suicide." Previously, it was estimated that a death by suicide profoundly affected six people, but that estimate has been raised to eighteen people. Our experience has been that suicide prevention is driven by survivors as many of them choose to get involved in suicide-prevention efforts. Scott Poland lost his father to suicide and now realizes he missed the warning signs. Suicide survivors have indicated that they received significant help when they participated in grief groups attended only by others who had lost loved ones to suicide—they sometimes felt out of place attending grief groups where participants who had lost loved ones due to other causes. Key school personnel such as counselors are encouraged to refer grieving students and families to the nearest suicide-survivor support group, although these groups can be found only in a few locations in Montana.

Section 1: Suicide Prevention
Section 1 includes guidelines for developing effective suicide-prevention programs for elementary schools, middle schools, and high schools. It will provide information on suicide awareness and strategies for the prevention of youth suicide. Staff development, student training, and information for parents will be discussed with specific recommendations for creating awareness and prevention training. Research has identified high-risk groups for youth suicide, which include American Indians, LGBT students, homeless students, students living in foster care, students with mental illness, students engaging in self-injury, incarcerated youth, and those bereaved of loved ones by suicide. In addition, we provide an overview of preventative information to post on the district website for suicide prevention.

Section 2: Suicide Intervention
Section 2 includes guidelines for developing effective assessment procedures for suicidal students at each educational level. We will discuss the development of safety plans and parent emergency notifications, the identification of internal and external resources, and re-entry guidelines for students returning from hospital. We have used the term "suicide-prevention specialist" or "expert" for the school districts. In many cases, that person will be a school counselor or school psychologist, but in smaller districts a school administrator—or even a lead teacher in the most isolated schools—may be conducting the initial suicide assessment with a student.

Section 3: Postvention After a Suicide
Section 3 includes guidelines for providing compassionate, honest, and effective responses in the event of a student's death by suicide. Postvention includes the responses needed for the family of the suicide victim, your school staff, your students, the community at-large, and the media. This section will provide step-by-step guidelines as it is recognized that postvention is a very challenging time for schools, and the primary purposes of postvention are to help students and staff with their emotions and to prevent further suicides. Adolescents are the most likely to imitate suicidal behavior, and suicide contagion is a process that can lead to suicide clusters. Carefully planned postvention responses are essential to prevent further suicides.

Tools for Schools

The Tools for Schools section is what makes this document a true toolkit. It provides sample forms that outline action steps that can be easily adapted and personalized with minor revisions to meet each school's or district's needs.

Appendices

Additional information can be found in the Appendices section, including answers to questions commonly asked by parents.

PREVENTION—INTERVENTION—POSTVENTION

Section 1: Suicide Prevention

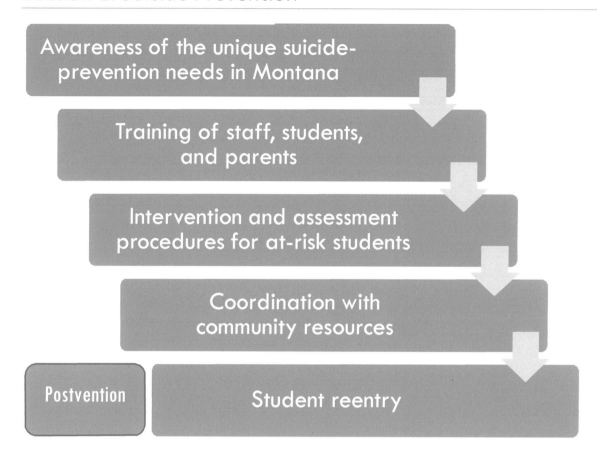

The Process for Developing Suicide-Prevention Programs

The Substance Abuse and Mental Health Services Administration (SAMHSA) recommends a four-step process for developing suicide-prevention programs in schools:

Step 1. Engage administrators, school boards, and other key players who will endorse the programmatic changes in the school and justify the time it takes to train school personnel and students. Administrators need to understand the scope of the problem, believe that suicide among our youth is unacceptable, realize that schools are the most logical places for students to be identified, and know that addressing suicidal ideation in students will not increase the risk. In short, administrators need to accept training for themselves and provide the leadership necessary to create a culture of suicide awareness and intervention expectations.

Step 2. Bring people together to start the planning process. Be sure to include the key players that will help promote suicide awareness and intervention. This would include school staff members and key community resources (e.g., suicide-prevention coalition members, clergy, cultural groups, and parent groups).

Step 3. Provide key players with basic information about youth suicide and suicide prevention.

Step 4. Develop your overall strategy for training staff/students and creating a culture of suicide awareness.

Key Components of a Model Policy for Suicide Awareness, Prevention, and Response

A model policy for suicide awareness, prevention, and response can best be developed by creating a suicide-prevention task force that includes community members, by reviewing local and state models, and by being familiar with best practices and evidence-based practices for suicide prevention in schools.

Locating and utilizing best-practice suicide-prevention programs in schools and identifying those that are evidence-based have been very challenging for school personnel. SAMHSA provides a National Registry of Evidence-based Programs and Practices (NREPP) for suicide prevention in schools. NREPP currently separates all existing programs into legacy programs and newly reviewed programs, and more information can be found at nrepp.samhsa.gov/AdvancedSearch.aspx It is important. Note that few programs are listed—only four in the newly reviewed category and ten in the legacy category.

The legacy category lists Sources of Strength and QPR Gatekeeper Training for Suicide Prevention, which are both recommended by the 2016 report by the Montana Suicide Mortality Review Team (MSMRT). The newly reviewed category includes Applied Suicide Intervention Skills Training and Signs of Suicide, which are both recommended by the MSMRT. The newly reviewed category also includes Kognito, which has been recommended by the Office of Public Instruction. MSMRT also recommends the use of the Good Behavior Game, which is technically not a suicide-prevention program but has research supporting its effectiveness in suicide prevention. Additionally, the MSRMT recommends Youth Aware of Mental Health.

Additional best-practice programs are the Youth Mental Health First Aid and programs from The Jason Foundation, which has numerous modules on suicide prevention and related issues. One of the authors of this toolkit is featured in five of those modules.

Schools are encouraged to contact OPI and DPHHS for recommendations and information about NREPP and best-practice programs and about the availability of low-cost and free programs. DPHHS has a suicide-prevention coordinator, and OPI has a coordinated health unit director.

Suicide-prevention information provided for staff and students should be selected very carefully and utilize best-practice programs. Schools are strongly encouraged to ensure that videos about suicide have been approved by the administration or curriculum director before they are shown. It is also strongly recommended that any speakers on the topic of suicide be researched carefully, and, ideally, that they have a background in the mental health field. School assemblies on suicide are not recommended due to the dramatic nature of bringing all students together; students will be very unlikely to ask questions, and it will be difficult to monitor their reactions. Suicide is best discussed in a classroom setting with the session led by a counselor or psychologist with the teacher present and invested in prevention.

Nothing is more important for a school district than to ensure the health, safety, and well-being of every student. Suicide is the second leading cause of death for school-age youth in Montana. Although Montana legislation House Bill 374, passed in 2015, only recommended training for school personnel, all staff should be trained on the warning signs of suicide annually. House Bill 381, passed in 2017, states districts shall have a crisis-response plan for suicide.

Model policies for suicide awareness, prevention, and response should include the following key components:

- Introduction and purpose
- Incidence of suicidal thoughts, suicide plans, suicide attempts, and deaths by suicide
- Consideration of at-risk populations within the school district, such as LGBTQ, bullying victims, bullies themselves, and students engaging in self-injury **(Tool 10: Overview of Additional Risk Factors Related to Suicidal Ideation)**
- Creation of a district suicide-prevention task force that cooperates with community resources
- Training and sharing of information with target groups, including staff, students, and parents, that provides suicide-prevention education and crisis resources (the Tools section includes numerous documents for educating each group)
- Assessment and identification processes that adhere to best-practice and evidence-based prevention programs as much as possible
- Parent notification **(Tool 18: Parent Acknowledgement Form for Student at Risk of Suicide)**
- Referral process that includes identified community resource providers that are well trained in suicide assessment and management **(Tool 16: Student Risk Report)**
- Procedures for responding to students at risk of suicide **(Tools 14A, 14B, 16, 17, and 18)**
- Reentry procedures for students who have been hospitalized **(Tool 20: Checklist for School Reentry)**
- Postvention procedures checklist **(Tool 21: Checklist for Postvention Steps)**
- Communication guidelines: leadership staff, students, parents, media, handbooks, website, etc. **(Tools 23, 24, 25, and 26; Appendix 2)**
- Documentation procedures for training of staff and for actions taken with students referred for being at risk of suicide **(Tools 5 and 8)**
- Concise overview of the plan for a district's policy on suicide awareness, prevention, and response **(Tool 6)**

Well-Trained Staff and Students

The importance of all school staff receiving training (which is recommended in Montana) on the warning signs of suicide and on the importance of referring at-risk students to the administration and counseling staff is the cornerstone of suicide prevention in schools. Additionally, the important development of depression screening helps students learn the warning signs of suicide and learn the importance of seeking help from adults when they realize that they or a friend are depressed and need to be immediately evaluated by a mental health professional. These important steps will result in more suicidal students being identified and referred for a suicide assessment. Each school needs key personnel trained in suicide assessment, and school counselors are the logical choice as they are typically based on only one campus. Erbacher, Singer, and Poland (2015) clarified that a suicide risk assessment is done to determine if suicidal ideation, intent, and plan are present and to identify what steps need to be taken to safeguard the student. A key part of the process is to determine if the student is at imminent risk (for example, in the next 48 hours). Miller (2011) stressed that no problem facing school mental health professionals is more urgent than the need for training in suicide assessment, and
that a good assessment results in an effective intervention. School personnel understandably experience anxiety when faced with a student who may be suicidal, and it is vital that they receive training in suicide assessment. This training can be provided by bringing experts to the school system to provide training in assessment and intervention or by sending key personnel to conferences and training

conducted by state and national associations that focus on suicide prevention, assessment, management, and postvention. Key personnel such as school administrators and counselors must also know the facts about youth suicide, and it is important that they not believe any of the myths about suicide. Recently, a school teacher asked, "Is it true that some students will die by suicide no matter what we do? Isn't it their destiny?" This is an example of why the recommended training in Montana is so important.

Additionally, it is very important to include positive examples of school personnel actions that resulted in a tragedy being averted. Uplifting examples are important to share as a way of recognizing that personnel can and have been about to identify suicidal students and provided appropriate services for them.

The Montana Suicide Mortality Review Team's 2016 report recommends a multi-level approach for all elementary and secondary students, utilizing best-practice programs and, whenever possible, those that have been identified as evidence-based interventions according to NREPP. MSMRT also recommends that all middle school student be screened for depression.

Ideally, it is important to provide training for all students for them to understand the warning signs of suicide and make referrals or seek self-help. While there are numerous training modules for staff and suicide task force members, only a few are available for students. This is an area that needs more development and can benefit from educators sharing activities and curriculum that works.

Available Training Programs

Question. Persuade. Refer. (QPR) is recommended for middle schools by the 2016 MSMRT report and involves gatekeeper training that teaches students and staff members how to identify risks and warning signs of suicide. Just as people trained in CPR and the Heimlich maneuver help save thousands of lives each year, people trained in QPR learn how to recognize the warning signs of a suicide crisis and how to question, persuade, and refer someone to help. Recommended for all levels of educational staff, including teachers, support staff, bus drivers, custodians, and food service personnel. www.qprinstitute.com/

Columbia Suicide Severity Rating Scale (C-SSRS; see Tools 14A and 14B) is recommended by the 2016 MSMRT report as an assessment tool to identify teens at risk for suicide and includes self-report questions about the student's general health and risk factors for suicide. www.cssrs.columbia.edu/

SOS Signs of Suicide is recommended for middle schools by the 2016 MSMRT report and is an effective intervention that educates students about suicide and how to identify suicide warning signs. mentalhealthscreening.org/programs/youth

Riding the Waves is a promising newly developed fifth-grade curriculum program from the state of Washington's Youth Suicide Prevention Program. crisisclinic.org/education/community-training-opportunities/school-curriculum/#RIDING

Youth Mental Health First Aid (YMHFA) teaches a five-step action plan to offer initial help to young people showing signs of a mental illness or in a crisis, and to connect them with the appropriate professional, peer, social, or self-help care. YMHFA is an eight-hour interactive training program for youth-serving adults without a mental health background. Recommended as a pilot project for high schools. www.mentalhealthfirstaid.org/cs/take-a-course/course-types/youth/ (Free YMHFA Training available through the CDE www.cde.ca.gov/ls/cg/mh/projectcalwell.asp)

Applied Suicide Intervention Skills Training (ASIST) is a two-day interactive workshop in suicide first aid. ASIST teaches participants to recognize when someone may have thoughts of suicide and to work with them to create a plan that will support their immediate safety. Recommended for all school counselors in middle schools and high schools. www.livingworks.net/programs/asist/

The PAX Good Behavior Game and the Good Behavior Game are two separate programs for early elementary school classes to teach children how to self-regulate emotions and behaviors. Both have been used with promising results in Montana. For tribal schools, the Indigenous version of the PAX Good Behavior Game is recommended. goodbehaviorgame.org/ www.air.org/goodbehaviorgame/

Youth Aware of Mental Health (YAM) is recommended by the 2016 MSMRT Report. It is a role-play curriculum that provides youth with an opportunity to enact real-life situations related to suicide and to focus on changing negative thoughts into positive coping skills. This program has also proven to be significant in decreasing bullying and substance abuse and in increasing help-seeking behavior. www.y-a-m.org/the-programme/

Kognito At-Risk is an evidence-based series of three interactive, online professional development modules designed for use by individuals, schools, districts, and statewide agencies. It includes tools and templates to ensure that the program is easy to disseminate and to use for measuring success at elementary, middle, and high school levels. www.kognito.com/products/pk12/

safeTALK is a half-day alertness training program that prepares anyone over the age of 15, regardless of prior experience or training, to become a suicide-alert helper. www.livingworks.net/programs/safetalk/

Training Goals

Training should be designed to achieve several specific goals related to suicide prevention.

Training Goals

All School Staff

Convey current statistics, beliefs, and attitudes about suicide in youth: ☐ Dispel myths ☐ Review protective factors for youth, including having programing that creates a suicide-awareness culture ☐ Stress never keeping a secret about a student's suicidal behavior, including cultivating a climate with connections between students and adults who are approachable and trusted Educate school staff to be prepared to recognize and respond to warning signs of suicide risk (Tools 9, 10, and 11) Provide information about suicide-prevention resources in your school and community	Promote the importance of intervention with at-risk youth and connect them with the needed help: ☐ Know the school referral procedures (Tool 8) ☐ Know who the suicide-prevention expert for the district or school is ☐ Know procedures to monitor students at risk of suicide (Tools 15A and 15B) Convey that suicide is almost always a preventable loss, and if a student died by suicide it was probably the result of untreated or undertreated mental illness Document staff attendance at suicide-prevention and -intervention training as recommended by the Montana Legislation (Tool 4) Document staff understanding of suicide prevention and intervention with a pre- and posttraining survey (Tool 5)

Additional training for suicide-prevention expert or specialist

Know how to implement suicide-assessment process (Tools 14A, 14B, 16, 17, 18, and 20)	Parent Acknowledgement Form for Student at Risk of Suicide (Tool 18)
Know how to monitor suicide risk using elementary/middle school version or the middle/high school version (Tools 15A and 15B)	Know how to implement strategies for reentry to school (Tool 20)
	Know how to implement postvention strategies (Tool 21 and Appendix 2)

Additional training for Principal and/or Administrators Serving in the Leadership Role

Communicating with staff in the aftermath of an attempted or completed suicide: ☐ Agenda for initial all-staff meeting (Tool 23)	☐ Providing teachers with information and guidance for working with shocked, confused, and grieving students (Tools 23 and 24) ☐ Working with the local media (Tools 25 and 26)

Elementary School Students	
PAX Good Behavior Game	Good Behavior Game
Secondary School Students	
Understanding suicide and recognizing the warning signs District/school procedures for receiving assistance for self or other(s)	SOS depression screening, Acknowledge Care Tell video, Sources of Strength, and YAM
Information for Parents	
Understanding suicide and recognizing the warning signs (Tools 9, 10, and 11) Answering parent questions and increasing their involvement (Tools 13 and 24; Appendix 1)	District/school procedures for obtaining assistance for suicidal student(s) both at school and in the community (Tool 29) Information about programs provided for students, such as Good Behavior Game, SOS, Sources of Strength, and YAM

Section 2: Suicide Intervention

How FERPA Applies to a Potentially Suicidal Student Intervention

One issue that school personnel struggle with is when and if they must notify parents in the event they believe a student to be suicidal.

> The only exception to notifying parents of a suicidal student is if abuse is suspected. In that case, the Montana Child and Family Services Division must be called.

It is important to note that while mental health personnel are to always uphold confidentiality, there are key exceptions to this rule. Suicidal ideation or behavior must be one of those exceptions.

The Family Educational Rights and Privacy Act (FERPA) prohibits a school from disclosing personally identifiable information from students' education records without the consent of a parent or eligible student, unless an exception to FERPA's general consent rule applies.

It is important to understand the exception to the FERPA rules when addressing the needs of a suicidal student as it is an emergency situation. Under this health or safety emergency provision, an educational agency or institution is responsible for determining whether to make a disclosure of personally identifiable information on a case-by-case basis, considering the totality of the circumstances pertaining to a threat to the health or safety of the student or others.

> If the school district or school determines that there is an articulable and significant threat to the health or safety of the student or other individuals, and that a party needs personally identifiable information from education records to protect the health or safety of the student or other individuals, it may disclose that information to such appropriate party without consent. 34 CFR § 99.36 (a).

This is a flexible standard under which the Department defers to school administrators, so that they may bring appropriate resources to bear on the situation, provided that there is a rational basis for the educational agency's or institution's decisions about the nature of the emergency and the appropriate parties to whom information should be disclosed. More information about this exception can be found at www2.ed.gov/policy/gen/guid/fpco/pdf/ferpa-disaster-guidance.pdf.

A challenging issue occurs if the student suspected of being suicidal is already 18 years of age. It is recommended that the parents of students who are 18 years or older be notified. The vast majority of parents will cooperate, and their children will be receptive to parent notification and recommendations from school personnel to keep their child safe.

In summary, all students should be aware of the limits of confidentiality, and that the school staff must notify the parents of a suicidal student. While it may upset the student that you are divulging their private information to their parents or other necessary school staff, it will be less difficult to repair rapport with a student who is alive than to deal with the potential outcomes if he/she does attempt or die by suicide without parent notification by the school staff of their concerns. One of the authors' experience has been that most suicidal students are actually relieved that help or a lifeline is being offered, and that many students know their parents will be supportive of their child getting the help they need. Almost all the liability cases against schools following the suicide of a student have been because the parents of a student known to be suicidal were not notified. The only exception to parent notification is when you have reason to believe the suicidal student is being abused by their parents, and then the call must be made immediately to the Montana Child and Family Services Division.

Treatment for the Student Who Is at Risk of Suicide

It is critical that staff, students, and parents be able to recognize the warning signs of a depressed and/or suicidal student. The training outlined earlier will certainly prepare the school staff to be alert and responsive to the needs of a distressed student. What we have not mentioned is the part that a student or parent plays in alerting the staff to warning signs and how to get assistance for their friend or loved one. Additional training for students, such as the SOS program, need to be conducted in the classroom, and parents should be educated about the warning signs and how to get help for their child.

The **Student Risk Report (Tool 16)** provides a compassionate and effective process for seeking assistance in averting a student death by suicide.

A referral to the counselor (who is likely the designated suicide-prevention expert) comes from a student, parent, or staff member. Sometimes, the student who is in distress will be the one to self- report. Many times, a friend, parent, or alert staff member will report the concern to the appropriate person. **Tool 8: The Response Procedures for Students at Risk of Suicide** identifies the important steps the counselor/suicide-prevention expert should take upon notification.

The designated suicide-prevention expert will conduct an assessment of the student to determine if he/she is at-risk **(Tools 14A and 14B)**, a safety plan will be developed with the student **(Tool 17)**, and notification to parents will be made **(Tool 18)**, followed by a conference and a referral to community mental health resources. See Tool 28 for a detailed list of questions to ask community mental health providers.

Community or regional mental health resources that have been identified prior to a suicidal crisis and explored and preapproved by district administration should be readily available **(Tool 31: Identification of Mental Health Facilities and Mental Health Providers)**.

Possible community mental health providers should be interviewed by phone to determine if they are trained in suicide assessment and management, and to determine that they have experience with school-age youth. The mental health provider enters into a cooperative relationship with the district/school and, with parent permission, must be willing to share appropriate information with designated school staff for the purpose of a smooth reentry to school.

A list of these providers will be compiled, so that it is readily available to the staff whose role it is to respond to students who are at risk of suicide and to make recommendations to parents.

Administrators, counselors, and the designated suicide-prevention expert must understand the importance of having a reentry procedure and monitoring of students **(Tool 20: Reentry Checklist; Tools**

15A and 15B: Suicide Risk Monitoring Tools). The teachers of a student at risk need to know that suicide is a concern, so they can be alert to further warning signs.

In the event a death by suicide cannot be prevented, postvention procedures are extremely critical for the benefit of the family, grieving students, and staff, and for educating the community about suicide prevention and intervention. Key messages are that no one thing or no one person is to blame. Administration will most certainly take the lead in this process as it is important to do so (see Section 3: Postvention After a Suicide).

School personnel have also frequently asked if all student threats of suicide need to be taken seriously and have commented that often a student is perhaps just seeking attention or is trying to manipulate a situation. The answer is that all student threats of suicide must be taken seriously even with elementary-age students, and the steps outlined below must be followed. It is certainly acknowledged that this will take a lot of time for key personnel such as school counselors, but taking all threats seriously and, most importantly, notifying their parents will save lives and also protect school personnel from liability should a suicide occur.

Creating a school suicide-prevention culture through an environment that promotes wellness, mental health, and connectedness; respects students; and honors students' emotional needs and academic needs will go a long way towards prevention of suicide. It's important for all students, staff, and parents to know how to get help for themselves or others should the suicide warning signs arise in an individual.

Assessment Procedures for the Suicidal Student

In this Montana CAST-S, a brief synopsis of recommended assessment procedures will be described with additional tools provided in the Tools section. **Key tools** provided are the following: Checklist for Reentry after Hospitalization (Tool 20), Suicide Risk Monitoring Tool (Tool 15A: Elementary/Middle School and Tool 15B: Middle/High School), Sample Safety Plan (Tool 17), Sample Parent Acknowledgement Form (Tool 18), Sample Risk Assessment Forms (Tools 14A and 14B), and the Student Suicide Risk Report (Tool 16).

The concepts for assessment of potential suicide is that inquiry must be direct, and rapport must be established with the student. **Direct inquiry will not plant the idea in the mind of a student!** Students are often ambivalent about suicide—one minute they may want to die and end what they believe to be unendurable pain, but the next minute there is a glimmer of hope, and something positive has

> It is essential to respond immediately when a student is believed to be suicidal

happened, and they want to live. The intervention of any one person can make all the difference, and many students, after being questioned about suicidal thoughts and plans, have felt relieved that someone is there to help them.

It is acknowledged that assessing students for suicidality results in considerable anxiety for the school personnel conducting the evaluation, and it is ideal to consult with a colleague during the assessment process. This can be accomplished by asking another staff member to sit with the student in question while the counselor makes a call to a colleague or supervisor for support and guidance.

> It is very important for Montana schools to provide training on suicide assessment for key personnel such as school counselors, and that training should include observing a role-play of assessing suicide risk with a student and a role-play of parent notification of their child's suicidal thoughts and/or behavior and referral to community-based services.

If training on suicide assessment is not available in the counselor's region of Montana, it is suggested that they conduct a role-play exercise with another staff member to increase their confidence. Counselors must also know how to take care of themselves emotionally, and tips for caregivers on managing their personal stress are in **Tool 27: Caring for the Caregiver**.

> The C-SSRS is free, appropriate for all ages, and has been translated into more than 100 languages.

A thorough interview with a suicidal student with excellent rapport established is essential, and standardized assessment scales can be a valuable addition to the interview as they have been published and validated by research. One nationally recommended scale, the Columbia-Suicide Severity Rating Scale **(C-SSRS; Tools 14A and 14 B)**, is already being utilized by school and hospital personnel in Montana with favorable reviews, and it is recommended by the 2016 MSMRT report. The brief version (14A) consists of six direct questions and is most applicable when a Montana administrator or teacher is making the assessment (if a school counselor is unavailable). The longer version (14B) includes the SAFE-T protocol and includes more questions and the identification of protective factors.

The C-SSRS website (cssrs.columbia.edu/) provides an overview of the CSSR-S and a link to a video on how to best utilize the instrument. Information about the scale is also available on the Montana DPHHS website, dphhs.mt.gov/suicideprevention/suicideresources.

In addition, SAMHSA provides a Suicide Safe App that can be downloaded free which provides directions for medical and mental health personnel on suicide assessment including case studies and the identification of risk and protective factors. More information about the Suicide Safe App is available at store.samhsa.gov/product/SAMHSA-Suicide-Safe-Mobile-App/PEP15-SAFEAPP1.

**Suicide assessment—which covers risk factors, warning signs, and protective factors for
suicidal students—can be determined by asking the following questions.**

What are the current feelings of the student?

What were the warning signs that initiated the referral? What is

the individual's current and past level of depression? What is

the student's current and past level of hopelessness?

Has the student currently, or in the past, thought about suicide (either directly or
passively)?

What was the method of any previous suicide attempt(s)?

Does the student have a current suicide plan or plan to harm him/herself?
(the more specific the plan, the higher the risk)

What method does he/she plan to use, and does the individual have access to the means?
(higher risk when either or both of those are affirmed)

What are the student's perceptions on burdensomeness and belongingness?

Have they been exposed to a suicide?

Do they have a history of engaging in Non-Suicidal Self-injury (NSSI), i.e. cutting or burning?

Is there a history of alcohol or drug use?

What are his/her current problems and stressors at home and at school?

Has the student demonstrated any abrupt changes in behaviors?

What is the student's current support system, and what protective factors are in place?
(higher isolation might indicate higher risk)

What is the student's current mental health status? Is there a history of mental illness?

Is there a history of bullying, victimization, loss, and/or trauma?
(any affirmative response might indicate a higher risk)

Has the student been exposed to other adverse childhood experiences, such as poverty;
physical, emotional, or sexual abuse; neglect; or living with a mentally ill relative, or have
they experienced significant losses of loved ones?

What are the student's reasons to live?
(healthy answers to this question might indicate lower risk)

The questions above and all rating scales are designed to help personnel such as school counselors identify the level of suicide risk for students.

There is only one exception to notifying parents when their child has had suicidal thoughts, and that is if the parents are believed to be abusing their child, in which case a call needs to be placed immediately to the Montana Child and Family Services Division. It is highly recommended that the parents of a student who is 18 years or older also be notified. It is anticipated that parents might be difficult to reach, and

> It is important that the parents of students who are assessed at low risk for suicide also be notified of the suicidal concern.

school personnel should keep the student suspected of being suicidal under close supervision until they can be transferred to their parents. If the parent simply cannot be reached, then school personnel need to work with local law enforcement and/or mental health personnel to secure the need of supervision for the student.

Safety Plans

Many generations of mental health professionals were taught to have suicidal clients/students sign a contract that they would not harm themselves. These contracts, referred to as no-suicide or no-harm contracts, were often preprinted on school stationery. Criticisms of these contracts were that mental health professionals might rush or even coerce a student into signing one. Miller (2011) emphasized that although the use of contracts is very widespread, there is no empirical research to support that contracts were effective in preventing suicide. Contracts also did not protect the professional from liability, and contracts were criticized for focusing on what the student would *not* do as opposed to what the student *would* do in a time of suicidal crisis to keep themselves safe.

Safety plans differ from no-suicide contracts in that they are not developed ahead of time. Instead, they are a tool developed jointly with the student in crisis. The safety plan focuses on identifying coping strategies and peer and adult support for the student, and it includes local and national suicide-prevention resources, hotline numbers, and crisis text lines. Students are given a copy of the plan they helped develop and are encouraged to review it when they have suicidal thoughts. Montana school personnel are strongly encouraged to follow effective practices and shift from the utilization of no- suicide contracts to the creation of safety plans with suicidal students. Montana DPHHS also provides safety-planning information and a sample safety plan at www.dphhs.mt.gov/amdd/suicide. A sample safety plan is also provided by the authors in **(Tool 17)**. Additionally, the Suicide Prevention Resource Center has a sample safety plan at www.sprc.org/sites/sprc.org/files/SafetyPlanTemplate.pdf.

Suicide Risk Levels and Required Action Steps

Low Risk (Ideation Only)

Develop a safety plan with the student Notify the parents of their child's suicidal ideation Document having parents sign an emergency notification form (Tool 18) Fill out the Suicide Risk Report (Tool 16)	Referral for community mental health treatment for the suicidal student and persuasively request that parents sign a release of information form, so that designated school personnel can directly communicate with community mental health professionals

Medium Risk (Current Ideation and Previous Suicidal Behavior)

Supervise student at all times (including rest rooms)
 	
Develop safety plan with the student
 	
Notify and release student **only** to:
 	
   ☐ Parent or guardian who agrees to increase supervision and seek immediate mental health assessment and treatment
   ☐ Law enforcement
   ☐ Psychiatric mobile responders or crisis team
 	
Utilize Suicide Risk Monitoring Tools (Tools 15A and B)
 	
Have parents sign a Parent Acknowledgement Form for Student at Risk of Suicide (Tool 18)
	Persuasively request that parents sign a release of information form, so that designated school personnel can speak directly with community mental health professionals
	
	Fill out the Suicide Risk Report (Tool 16)
	
	Develop follow-up plan at school that includes a reentry plan if the student is hospitalized. All students returning from mental health hospitalization should have a reentry meeting where parents, school, and community mental health personnel make appropriate follow-up plans to support the student prior to going to class

High Risk (Current Plan and Access to Method)

Supervise student at all times (including rest rooms)
 	
Develop safety plan with the student
 	
Notify and release student **only** to:
 	
   ☐ Parent or guardian who commits to increase supervision and seek immediate mental health assessment and treatment
   ☐ Law enforcement
   ☐ Psychiatric mobile responders or crisis team
 	
Persuasively request that parent sign a release of information form, so that designated school personnel can speak directly with community mental health professionals
	Document all actions, including having parents sign a Parent Acknowledgement Form for Student at Risk of Suicide (Tool 18)
	
	Fill out the Suicide Risk Report (Tool 16)
	
	Develop follow-up plan at school that includes a reentry plan if the student is hospitalized. All students returning from mental health hospitalization should have a reentry meeting where parents, school, and community mental health personnel make appropriate follow-up plans to support the student prior to returning to class
	
	Utilize Suicide Risk Monitoring Tools (Tools 15A and 15B)

Notifying Parents of Child at Risk of Suicide

Parents are key to helping the suicidal student, and school districts have been successfully sued by parents who were not notified of their child's suicidal behavior. The following suggestions are offered for engaging and supporting parents of a suicidal student. It is strongly suggested that a conference with parents be held in person rather than via the telephone, and that a suicidal student not be allowed to leave school on their own even if that is what his/her parents have requested. **Tool 19** contains detailed information on how to engage in an in-person conference.

Transfer of Responsibilities to Parents: Notification and Making the Call

Failure of the school to notify parents/guardians when there is reason to suspect that the student is suicidal is the most common source for lawsuits. If there is reason to believe that a student is contemplating suicide, the parents must be notified. Several lawsuits—including one that one of the authors of this report is currently involved in—were situations where a peer told the school counselor that their friend was suicidal, but the parents of the student were not notified, and the student died by suicide a week or two later. The school counselor in the current case interviewed the student suspected of being suicidal but chose not to contact the parents and is currently being sued.

> School personnel have an obligation to notify the parents of any student who is suspected to be at risk for suicide, even if the information received is second-hand and the student suspected of being suicidal denies it.

The challenge for school personnel is to get a supportive reaction from parents, increase supervision of the student, and obtain needed mental health services for the student.

In the event the parents are believed to be abusive, or if they refuse to obtain recommended mental health treatment in the community, then Montana Child and Family Services Division should be notified.

If the parents are uncooperative and refuse to come to the school to talk and/or personally pick up their child, school staff cannot allow a suicidal student to walk home or take transportation home regardless of parent directive. A Maryland school district settled out of court with the parents of a student who died by suicide who was allowed to walk home at parent request after the school notified the parents that the student was suicidal. Parents or a guardian must pick up the child and engage in a conference with the designated school staff member, who will provide details of school assessment and community mental health resources. If parents emphatically refuse to come to school, then law enforcement, Montana Child and Family Services Division, and mobile crisis teams need to be notified and utilized.

Community Resources

School counselors would likely be the appropriate personnel to follow up with the family and student to inquire if outside services are being rendered, but it is noted that an administrator or even a teacher in the most isolated and smallest districts of Montana may need to fulfill this role. It is strongly recommended that a counselor or psychologist on the school staff be identified as the suicide- prevention specialist or expert. It is also strongly recommended that a release of information form be signed by the parents to allow the school counselor to communicate with outside practitioners, such as therapists and medical personnel. Parents may be reluctant to sign a release of information form, and school counselors are encouraged to explain thoroughly and persuasively why it is in the best interest of the student for the release to be signed, so that information may be shared.

One of the challenges for school personnel and especially school counselors or designated suicide-prevention specialists or experts is to refer suicidal students to private practitioners, agencies, and hospitals where the professionals are well trained in suicide assessment and management. A parent once commented to one of the authors of this report, "I took my son to a psychologist in the community as the school recommended but was told by the psychologist not to worry as my son was exhibiting typical teenage behavior, and two weeks later he died by suicide." A task force of the American Association of Suicidology addressed serious gaps in the training of mental health providers concerning suicide assessment (Schmitz, Allen, Feldman, Gutin, Jahn, Kleespies, Quinett & Simpson, 2012). The task force called for accrediting bodies, training programs, and licensing organizations to improve training through coursework and required continuing education and to include examination questions for licensure to improve competency in suicide assessment. Few changes are expected in the near future to address the lack of training that most mental health professionals have in suicide assessment, but Montana school counselors should refer to professionals that they know are well trained and competent in suicide assessment and management. This example is an illustration of why every school district needs to screen, approve, and compile a list of well-trained health care providers prior to a student being identified as at risk. The potential health care providers need to be asked questions about their training and experience in suicide assessment and management, especially with a school-age client. Key questions to ask the potential health care providers can be found in **Tool 28: Screen Mental Health Providers**. **Tool 32: Memorandum of Understanding** will assist school personnel to ensure that communication and collaboration between schools and outside mental health services are coordinated. Remember that the district is not responsible for the cost of a suicidal student undergoing outside assessment and treatment. The parent acknowledgement form signed by the parent will reinforce this practice **(Tool 18)**.

Student Reentry After Hospitalization for Suicidal Behavior

The reentry process and follow-up procedures after hospitalization for a student who has expressed the desire to end his/her life by suicide are essential, and the student should be considered at high risk immediately upon reentering their school environment. It is critical that key school personnel such as the counselor or the suicide-prevention expert carefully monitor the student's suicidal behavior as there is a great need for continuing mental health care and assessment of suicide risk. This can best be done by utilizing the **Suicide Monitoring Tools provided in Tools 15A and 15B**. The counselor should review the **Reentry Checklist (Tool 20)** as they address with the student and his/her parents the following considerations:

- The student may have fallen behind on the curriculum that is important for graduating or passing to the next grade. Empathy and compassion should be shown in this situation. Academic expectations for lessons that were missed should be adjusted to allow for extended time for assignments, possible modification of assignments, and a notation of "incomplete" for the term until the prioritized work has been turned in and assessed.
- The suicidal student's teachers need to know that depression and suicide are of concern. Discussion as to why the student has been suicidal and discussions of possible contributing

factors such as losses, family issues, mental illness, or bullying are to be avoided. The emphasis should be on teachers simply acknowledging depression and suicide as a concern and knowing the importance of being alert to further warning signs of suicide. In the event the teacher becomes concerned about a student's suicidal behavior, the teacher should escort the student to the counseling office for immediate attention.

- It is recommended that key school personnel such as counselors meet weekly for a minimum of a month with a student returning from hospitalization due to suicidal behavior and utilize the **Suicide Risk Monitoring Tools (Tool 15A for elementary/middle school students and Tool 15B for middle/high school students)**. Suicide assessment is not a single event but necessitates careful follow-up at school and coordination with community mental health providers.

Section 3: Postvention After a Suicide

In the event that a student suicide has occurred in your student population, those who are in contact with community, parents, students, and extended district services must respond in an empathetic and factual way. The suicide of a student likely will have an effect far beyond the school that they attended as vulnerable youth find each other through social media. Research has also found that school postvention efforts were often too short and focused on too few students. The information in **Tool 21** will provide steps for schools to follow after a suicide. It is strongly recommended that administrators review these documents prior to losing a student to suicide, but it is essential that they review them prior to making decisions after the suicide of a student. Shneidman cited by Poland (1989) defined postvention as a series of helpful acts after a dire event, and he stressed that assisting survivors of suicide (those that lost a loved one to suicide) may be the greatest mental health challenge of our time. Postvention activities in schools focus on helping everyone with their shock, grief, confusion, and even guilt. A primary goal of postvention is to prevent further suicides as, unfortunately, adolescents are the most prone to imitate suicidal behavior, and suicide contagion has led to suicide clusters in a number of school communities. The U.S. Department of Education has provided grants to several school districts that experienced suicide clusters. More information about Project SERV grants is available here: www2.ed.gov/programs/dvppserv/index.html.

The first *After a Suicide: Toolkit for Schools* was published in 2011 (by www.afsp.org and www.sprc.org) and is the most concise guide that has ever been written for schools at a challenging time. It is posted at the Montana DPHHS website, www.dphhs.mt.gov/amdd/suicide. The guide will answer almost any question educators might have about how to respond to a suicide in the school community, and Montana educators are strongly encouraged to download and utilize the guide. As one of the authors of the Montana toolkit, Dr. Scott Poland was a contributor to the *After a Suicide Toolkit* and is currently working on revisions to the toolkit, which is expected to be released in the fall of 2017. Few changes are expected, but additional information will be provided about suicide contagion and social media.

Critical Procedures to Follow in the Aftermath of a Death by Suicide

Postvention has become synonymous with the challenging aftermath of suicide, and few events are scarier for a school, its staff, its students, and the community than a youth suicide. The tasks at hand include helping students and staff members to manage their feelings of shock, grief, and confusion. The major focus should be grief resolution and prevention of further suicides. A **postvention checklist is available in Tool 21**, which includes information on how to approach difficult duties such as contacting the parents, notifying staff and students, and arranging a memorial. More information is also available in "After a Suicide: Postvention for Schools" by Dr. Scott Poland and Richard Lieberman (Appendix 2) and under the publications section at www.nova.edu/suicideprevention.

TOOLS FOR SCHOOLS

Tool 1: Leadership Involvement—Recommended District Action Steps

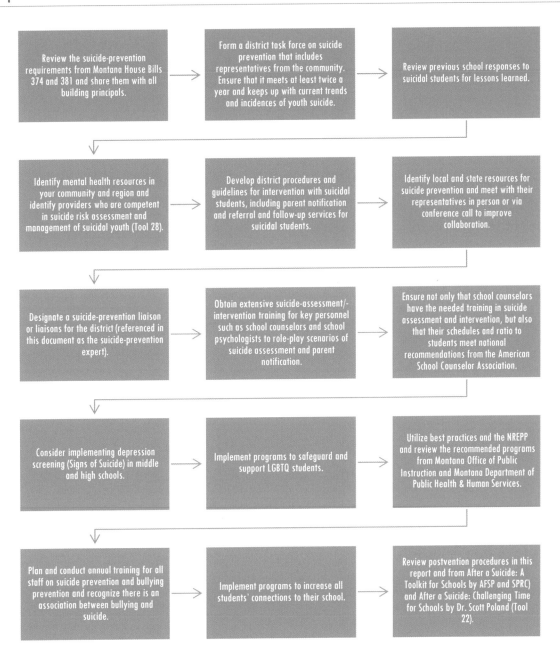

Action Steps to Promote a Suicide-Prevention Culture

Create policy memos regarding training and intervention expectations for staff regarding suicide awareness.

Disseminate messages from administrative leaders across the district/school.

Instruct administrative leadership to address suicide prevention at least once per year during in-service opportunities.

Make district/schools leadership aware of student suicide risk assessment and procedures in order to encourage early help-seeking behavior.

Ensure that leadership in the smallest and most isolated Montana schools where no counselors are available are comfortable using the brief version of the C-SSRS for suicide assessment (Tool 14A).

Tool 2: Recommended Leadership Involvement Checklist

Provide suicide-prevention training as recommended by Montana legislation and based on best practices and on recommendations by NREPP. Professional training conducted at district and school levels should include all staff identified by the MSMRT Report.

Main Personnel

Administrators, counselors, psychologists, SROs, nurses, crisis-response designees.

Teachers and teaching assistants (classroom professionals).

Office support staff, such as secretaries and attendance clerks.

Strongly Recommended Additional Personnel

Ancillary staff: custodians, cafeteria workers, bus drivers and attendants, and part-time staff such as coaches and arts teachers.

Training Recommendations

Training should be conducted by mental health personnel for administrators and crisis-response designees on the use of mental health services.

Administrators and crisis-response designees receive suicide-prevention and -intervention training at least once per year. Every classroom professional must receive this training once per year.

Staff entering mid-year or after training has been conducted must be provided training upon employment.

Time spent on suicide-prevention training and activities must be documented.

A pre- and post-training survey (Tool 5) is recommended for identifying the degree of understanding of and confidence in implementing a suicide-awareness culture.

All school personnel who have accomplished the recommended annual suicide-prevention training must be documented Tool 4).

All parents have been provided access to the suicide-prevention information and the district/school intervention and response information that is posted on the district website (Tool 29).

All supervisory personnel with student interaction have completed suicide-prevention and -intervention training.

Student suicide-prevention information promoting prescribed response and listing resources on suicide-prevention lifelines has been reviewed and discussed according to age appropriateness.

Procedures for Screening and Identification of Depression

All crisis-response designees have been educated about the district/school prevention and response procedures and about parent permission procedures, and they have considered the use of depression screening with secondary students. More secondary students will be able to participate in depression screening if passive parental permission procedures are utilized.

Crisis Response Team:

The district/school has access to a fully trained Crisis Response Team.

The district/school has documented and shared with the school community the staff roles in the suicide-prevention and -intervention process.

Communication of Information about Suicide Prevention and Intervention
Information for the school board (Tool 6 offers an overview of the concise policy).
Information on district/school website (Tool 29).
Letters to staff, students, parents, and local mental health resources.
Campus improvement plan (samples provided in Tools 7A and 7B).
Meetings with faculty, students, parents, and local resources.
Documentation
Monitored suicide statistics, tracked suicide-prevention training, and ensured full implementation of the suicide-prevention efforts.

Tool 3: Checklist for Effective School-Based Suicide-Prevention Programs

Montana schools are encouraged to use NREPP and best practices prevention programs and to contact Montana OPI and DPHHS for recommendations on programs. As identified by best practices, Montana OPI, Montana DPHHS, and SAMHSA, effective training designed by local administrators should achieve several specific goals related to suicide prevention:
Convey current statistics, beliefs, and attitudes about youth suicide. ☐ Dispel myths about suicide ☐ Identify protective factors ☐ Stress the importance of never keeping secret a student's suicidal behavior
Educate school staff to be prepared to recognize and respond to warning signs of suicide risk.
Promote the importance of intervention with suicidal youth and connect them with the needed help. ☐ Know the school response procedures (Tool 8) ☐ Know who the suicide-prevention specialist is
Provide information about mental health and prevention resources in your community.
Review the information posted about suicide prevention on the district website (Tool 29).
Convey that suicide is almost always preventable.
Document staff attendance and understanding through pre- and postsurveys.
Helpful resources
American Association of Suicidology: www.suicidology.org
American Foundation for Suicide Prevention: www.afsp.org
Center for Disease Control and Prevention: www.cdc.gov
National Alliance on Mental Illness: www.nami.org
Suicide Awareness Voices of Education: www.save.org
The Jason Foundation: www.jasonfoundation.com
The Trevor Project: www.trevorproject.org
Nova Southeastern University Suicide- and Violence-Prevention Office: www.nova.edu/suicideprevention
Society for the Prevention of Teen Suicide: www.sptsusa.org
SAMHSA's National Registry of Evidence-based Programs and Practices: www.samhsa.gov/nrepp

Tool 4: Template for Documentation of Training

Completion of Suicide-Prevention Training					
Name	ID #	Suicide Awareness	Suicide Assessment		

Staff-development hours documented by: _____Date: _____

Tool 5: Pre- and Posttraining Survey

The purpose of this survey is to collect information regarding your understanding about youth suicide and your confidence in identifying and knowing what to do in the event a student expresses suicidal ideation.

Please check the descriptor that most reflects your opinion and/or understanding based on your experiences. A comment space has been provided for additional information, should you wish to elaborate on your response.

Name:			ID#: _ Date:	
1	2	3	Agree=1, Somewhat Agree=2, Disagree=3	Comments
			1. Suicide rates have increased for adolescents.	
			2. Discussing suicide with a student may increase his/her risk of attempting suicide.	
			3. Suicide is largely inherited and unavoidable.	
			4. Suicide often occurs on a whim and without much forethought.	
			5. Suicidal individuals do not make plans for the future.	
			6. A successful student with lots of friends would not take his/her life by suicide.	
			7. There are often no warning signs before a student takes his/her life by suicide.	
			8. I am confident that I can identify suicide warning signs in my students.	
			9. I know who to refer a suicidal student to in my school.	
			10. I have received suicide-awareness training.	
			11. I am aware of the suicide-prevention culture in our schools.	
			12. I understand the Suicide Risk Assessment and Safety Chart.	
			13. Suicide-prevention policies and procedures are clear in my school district.	
			14. I feel I have received enough training/information on identifying a student with suicidal ideation to alert the appropriate staff.	

Guidelines for the Instructor
Additional questions can be added.

Desired answers: 1-Agree, 2-Disagree, 3-Disagree, 4-Disagree, 5-Disagree, 6-Disagree, 7-Disagree, 8-Agree, 9-Agree, 10-Agree, 11-Agree, 12-Agree, 13-Agree, 14-Agree

Tool 6: Recommended District Plan for Suicide Prevention, Intervention, and Postvention

Prevention

School staff—including teachers, administrators, counselors, psychologists, social workers, nurses, secretaries, custodians, bus drivers, and cafeteria workers—are trained annually on suicide prevention. Training includes warning signs, commonly held myths and district referral procedures in accordance with the recommended programs from OPI, DPHHS, and the Montana CAST-S. It is recognized that all educators have a responsibility to work together to prevent youth suicide, and that youth suicide is largely the result of untreated or undertreated mental illness. We recognize that youth suicide prevention is a shared responsibility between schools and the community, and that good training and planning in schools will decrease the stigma surrounding suicide and result in the identification of suicidal students.

Intervention

The district provides training for key personnel such as counselors, psychologists, nurses, and social workers on conducting a suicide assessment for students suspected of being at risk for suicide. In accordance with recommendations provided by OPI, DPHHS, and Montana CAST-S, risk assessment includes parent notification and referral to community-based mental health services even if the suicide risk is rated as low. Parent notification will be documented, utilizing forms provided in Montana CAST-S. Follow-up services and monitoring at school will be provided for all students suspected of being suicidal, regardless of the risk level. A reentry meeting will be conducted for any student returning from hospitalization.

Postvention

If a student suicide occurs, it is recognized as a challenging and very sad time for his/her family, friends, and school. The best-practice postvention procedures outlined in the Montana CAST-S and *After a Suicide: A Toolkit for Schools* (2017) from the American Foundation for Suicide Prevention (www.afsp.org) and the Suicide Prevention Resource Center (www.sprc.org) will be utilized to guide all school and district efforts to support staff, students, and parents in dealing with their shock, grief, and confusion. The district recognizes that, after a suicide, an increasing number of students will have thoughts of suicide, and best practices postvention in schools reduces the likelihood that further suicide will occur.

Tool 7: Campus Improvement Plan Example with Suggested Goals

Addressing Montana HB 374 and HB 381				
HB 374/HB 381 Directives	District/School Goal	District/School Activities	Implementation/ Completion Dates	Documentation of Implementation/Completion
OPI will provide guidance, technical assistance, and training materials to schools on youth suicide awareness and prevention.	The district/school will provide Montana's CAST-S materials to all elementary, middle, and high schools. The district/school will collaborate with OPI, seeking guidance, technical assistance, and training.	1a. Obtain CAST-S materials. 1b. Distribute at least one copy to each campus location and identify the location where materials will be maintained. 2a. Conduct regular meetings in person or by phone conference to seek guidance throughout the year. 2b. Determine technical assistance needs for ongoing training and request support and/or funding, as necessary. 2c. Establish an in-service professional-growth training schedule that enables staff members to receive the required training.	TBD by school/district in collaboration with OPI.	1a. OPI/district roster indicating receipt of training. 1b. District list of campuses and locations where materials are maintained. 2a. Calendar documentation and notes from meetings. 2b. Documentation of meeting(s) held with representative team members and requests made to OPI for technical assistance. 2c. In-service sign-in logs, samples of training materials, videos of training, etc.

HB 374/HB 381 Directives	District/School Goal	District/School Activities	Implementation/ Completion Dates	Documentation of Implementation/Completion
School district employees who work directly with students are encouraged to complete at least one hour of training on youth suicide awareness and prevention annually.	A designated suicide-prevention expert will be trained on suicide awareness, prevention, intervention, and postvention. The district/school will mandate that each employee receive one hour of training on youth suicide awareness and prevention each year.	1a. A counselor, psychologist, or administrator will be identified at each campus location. 1b. The designated suicide-prevention expert will receive comprehensive training from national-/state-level suicide expert(s). 2a. All administrators, teachers, teacher assistants, support staff, custodians, food service workers, and bus drivers will receive one hour of training annually. 2b. All new staff will receive training upon employment or before the school year begins.	TBD by school/district in collaboration with OPI.	1a. District roster identifies individual for each campus. 1b. Suicide-prevention expert will provide campus administrator with evidence of attendance at formal training from national-/state-level suicide expert(s). 2a. In-service sign-in logs, training agenda, samples of training materials, pre- and postsurveys, videos of training, etc. 2b. Sign-in logs, training agenda, samples of training materials, pre- and postsurveys, videos of training, etc.

Tool 8: Response Procedures for Student at Risk of Suicide

Referral from Student, Parent, or School Staff

School Suicide-Prevention Expert

- Meets with student
- Assesses risk through direct inquiry
- Recommends removal of lethal means
- Develops safety plan and provides crisis hotline
- Notifies parents and requests a face-to-face conference immediately
- Monitors student closely until parent(s) arrive
- Documents all steps taken
- Refers to community resources. Note: If parents are uncooperative and refuse to get help, refer to Child and Family Services Division

Community Resources

- Provides a preidentified/-approved list of well-trained community providers and available resources
- Encourages treatment by community provider
- Parent provides release form for community provider to share information with school suicide-prevention expert

School Suicide-Prevention Expert

- Conducts a reentry meeting with student and parent(s)
- Conducts a reentry meeting with appropriate staff if student missed school or was hospitalized
- Ensures school staff and especially teachers are alert to future warning signs of suicide
- Follow-up daily/weekly, face-to-face (depending on severity but minimum weekly)

Tool 9: Common Myths About Youth Suicide

Montana educators must address the many myths about suicide in order to increase prevention efforts. It is essential that educators know the facts and not hold on to myths. A more detailed list of myths with deeper explanations of the corresponding facts is available in the e-resources for *Suicide in Schools: A Practitioner's Guide to Multi-level Prevention, Assessment, Intervention, and Postvention*: www.routledge.com/Suicide-in-Schools-A-Practitioners-Guide-to-Multi-level-Prevention-Assessment/Erbacher-Singer-Poland-Mennuti-Christner/p/book/9780415857024

Common Myths

Myth: If I ask a student about suicidal ideation, I will put the idea in his or her head.

Fact: Asking someone about suicide will not make him or her suicidal. In fact, if the student is suicidal, it provides an opportunity for the student to unburden him- or herself and learn sources of assistance. If the student is not having suicidal thoughts, then the conversation provides an opportunity to talk about what to do if the student or a friend ever does have suicidal thoughts.

Myth: There is a single cause or a simple reason for a youth suicide.

Fact: The suicide of a young person is very complex and the result of many factors, and the student has often traveled a long road, had significant mental health problems, and experienced many traumatic events.

Myth: If a student really wants to die by suicide, there is nothing I can do about it.

Fact: Suicide is preventable. Even students at the highest risk for suicide are still ambivalent about desiring death and desiring life. Most of all, they want things to change.

Myth: Students who talk about suicide all the time are not actually suicidal; therefore you don't need to take the statements seriously.

Fact: Youth who make suicidal statements typically have some risk for suicide. About 80% to 90% of people who died by suicide expressed their intentions to one and often more than one person. All suicidal statements should be taken seriously.

Myth: Suicide usually occurs without warning.

Fact: A person planning suicide usually gives clues about his or her intentions, although, in some cases, the clues may be subtle.

Myth: A suicidal person fully intends to die.

Fact: Most suicidal people feel ambivalent toward death and arrange an attempted suicide at a place and time in the hope that someone will intervene.

Myth: Suicidal individuals do not make future plans.

Fact: Many individuals who died by suicide had future plans; for example, they had planned activities and trips.

Myth: Those who died by suicide almost always left a note.

Fact: About 75% of suicide victims did not leave a note.

Myth: Young people engaging in self-injury—such as moderate superficial cutting or burning their body—will not attempt suicide.

Fact: Young people engaging in self-injury may acquire the ability for a suicide attempt as they become comfortable and habituated to harming themselves.

Myth: If a person attempts suicide once, he or she remains at constant risk for suicide throughout life.

Fact: Suicidal intentions are often limited to a specific period, especially if help is sought and received.

Myth: If a person shows improvement after a suicidal crisis, the risk has passed.

Fact: Most suicides occur within three months or so after the onset of improvement when the person has the energy to act on intentions, say goodbyes, and put their affairs in order.

Myth: Suicide occurs most often among the very rich and the very poor.

Fact: Suicide occurs in equal proportions among persons of all socioeconomic levels.

Myth: Families can pass on a predisposition to suicidal behavior.

Fact: Suicide is not an inherited trait but an individual characteristic resulting from a combination of many variables. One variable may be that another family member has died by suicide, creating exposure to suicide, and there may be a history of depression in the family.

Myth: All suicidal persons are mentally ill, and only a psychotic person will commit suicide.

Fact: Studies of hundreds of suicide notes indicate that suicidal persons are not necessarily mentally ill.

Myth: If a suicidal individual is stopped from using one method, he or she will find another way to die by suicide.

Fact: Research has documented that, if a specific method is removed and unavailable, suicidal individuals are very unlikely to seek another method. The Means Matter website at Harvard provides extensive research that removing the lethal means, such as a gun, and raising the barrier on bridges have decreased suicides. More information is available at www.hsph.harvard.edu/means-matter.

Tool 10: Overview of Additional Risk Factors Related to Suicidal Ideation

Depressed Youth

Research has found that approximately 20% of all teenagers suffer from depression at some point during their adolescence, and most do not receive treatment. While experiencing depression doesn't mean suicidal ideation is imminent for every student, it is the most common indicator in suicidal youth. Students may appear irritable, tearful, down, or sullen and not find pleasure in the activities they previously enjoyed. The key to distinguishing depression from normal teenage behavior is whether it is persistent over a period of several weeks and perseverant, meaning that it affects all aspects of their life (academic, social, and family). Younger children may express depression through somatic complaints, such as headaches, bad feelings in the stomach, etc. School personnel should be trained on the incidence of depression, be alert to students' shifting moods, and access community mental health resources. It is particularly important to pay attention to themes of hopelessness and depression in the writing and artwork of students and to alert key personnel, such as counselors and administrators, when such themes are noted.

Precipitating Events

Precipitating events have been referred to as the "straw that broke the camel's back," meaning that the student was previously suicidal, and that one more thing they cannot cope with on top of everything else has caused them to act on their previously thought-out suicide plans. School personnel should be alert to the following stressful events, which might trigger a suicide attempt: romantic breakup, severe argument with family or friends, recent loss of a loved one (including a pet), victim of bullying or severe humiliation, school failure, loss of a dream (such as not making a school team or being rejected from college of choice), severe school discipline, or arrest/incarceration. It is important that school personnel be alert to all of these precipitating events but especially to students in serious disciplinary trouble as some parents whose children died by suicide, and whose children received punishment by school administration for serious infractions, have claimed the punishment to be a contributing factor to their children's suicide. If a student is being expelled from school, it is recommended that the school offer counseling immediately before the student leaves the campus.

Relationship Between Bullying and Suicide

The media coined the term "bullycide" as a means to strongly imply that the bullying that the victim received was the causation for his/her suicide. Students involved in bullying—as the victim or the bully—are at a significantly higher risk for depression and suicide. Furthermore, the more frequently an adolescent was involved in bullying, the more likely it is that he or she was depressed, had feelings of hopelessness, had serious suicidal ideation, or had attempted suicide. Internalizing problems (including withdrawal, anxiety, and depression), having low self-esteem, displaying low assertiveness, and showing aggressiveness early in childhood (possibly due to rejection by peers and/or social isolation) are personal characteristics that increase a youth's likelihood of being bullied as well as the risk factors for suicidality. Further, LGBTQ students are often stigmatized and bullied in school, and they are more likely to attempt suicide. Knowing the frequency of bullying in schools and knowing these statistics that illustrate the connection between bullying and suicide, it only makes sense for schools to thoroughly screen for suicidal thoughts/behaviors when addressing bullying incidents and/or through bullying-prevention programs (www.sprc.org/resources-programs/suicide-bullying-issue-brief).

Non-Suicidal Self-Injury

The most common forms of non-suicidal self-injury (NSSI) are cutting, burning, and scratching the skin and not letting wounds heal. NSSI incidences have increased for youth, and the primary theories on NSSI explain that they engage in this behavior to release endorphins or to regulate emotions. NSSI is a complex coping behavior that fulfills a multitude of needs for those that engage in it. NSSI is a strong predictor of suicide as students are essentially practicing harming themselves, and schools need to develop training and protocols for staff to help them better understand and respond to NSSI, and key personnel such as school counselors need to be familiar with the most effective treatments.

Adverse Childhood Experiences

Approximately one-third of adults who were physically abused in their childhood have seriously considered taking their own life—a rate that is five times higher than adults who were not physically abused in their childhood. The research suggests suicide may have developmental origins relating to abuse—that physical or sexual abuse may lead to changes in the stress response in the brain, which increases the risk of suicidal thoughts and behavior. Other key factors for adverse childhood experiences for youth include living in poverty, neglect, parental rejection, living in foster care, emotional abuse, loss of a parent, and living with a mentally ill or substance-abusing family members. Students who have adverse childhood experiences need a great deal of support and continuing mental health care.

Sleep Deprivation in Adolescents

A growing body of research well documents that many adolescents are sleep deprived. Even though adolescents require as much as eight to ten hours of sleep at night, according to the National Sleep Foundation they simply are not wired to retire early to bed and have difficulty falling asleep before 11 p.m., and cell phone calls and messages may awaken them during the night. The majority of secondary schools in the US begin as early as 7:30 a.m. Numerous studies have addressed the harmful effects of sleep deprivation on adolescents and found a significant relationship between sleep deprivation and suicide completion for adolescents. One author of this report responded to suicide clusters in both Fairfax County and Palo Alto communities, and many community concerns were voiced about the lack of sleep for adolescents as a contributing factor to depression, hopelessness, and suicide. The Fairfax County Schools changed the start time for high schools to 8:00 a.m. or later.

Learning-Disabled Youth

Students with learning disabilities (LD) are well acquainted with academic difficulty and maladaptive academic behavior. In comparison to students without LD, they exhibit elevated levels of learned helplessness, including diminished persistence, lower academic expectations, and negative affect. Social behavioral research has indicated there is an increased risk for suicide among students with LD that is linked to depression, feelings of hopelessness, and isolation/rejection from the mainstream.

Cultural Factors

Culture is an important dynamic in the thoughts of a suicidal student, in the approach used with their family, and in any resources that might be recommended. Particularly in the aftermath of a death by suicide, school personnel should be sensitive to the cultural beliefs of the family and the student population, and great care should be taken to seek out personnel and resources that are a good match for the needs of the family during intervention and/or postvention. It should especially be noted that American Indian youths have a high suicide rate, and Montana educators need to be very familiar with tribal customs and practices.

Impact of Experiences and Personal Resiliency

A young person develops the feelings of self-worth, control, and positivity through a sum total of the events and experiences in his/her life. Covey emphasized that students have an emotional bank account. When good things happen, such as good grades, friendships, and engaging activities, chips are placed in the emotional bank account. When bad things happen, such as bad grades, breakups with friends, isolation, and death of friend or family member, chips are withdrawn. Research reflects that a young person's ability to bounce back from trauma or stress, to adapt to changing circumstances, and to respond positively to difficult situations is proportional to their resilience. Research has found that the keys to resiliency for youth are being surrounded by caring and supportive family and friends, remaining optimistic about the future, utilizing problem-solving skills, and having the opportunity to vent strong emotions. On the opposite end of the spectrum is the student who has a diminished sense of self-worth, has an inability to cope, is socially withdrawn, is unable to handle life stressors, and lacks a support network. Family and school environments that are supportive and caring will enhance resilience, while lack of family support or exposure to abuse or trauma may make a student vulnerable.

Protective Factors that Decrease Suicidal Behavior

The World Health Organization lists a number of factors that can decrease suicidal behavior, see below. More information can be found here:

www.who.int/mental_health/prevention/suicide/suicideprevent/en/

- Family cohesion and stability
- Coping and problem-solving skills
- Positive self-worth and impulse control
- Positive connections to school and extracurricular participation
- Successful academically
- Good relationships with other youth
- Seeks adult help when needed
- Lack of access to suicidal means
- Access to mental health care
- Religiosity
- School environment that encourages help seeking and promotes health
- Early detection and intervention

Tool 11: Facts About Suicide and Mental Disorders in Adolescents

From: *After a Suicide: A Toolkit for Schools*

Suicide is not inexplicable and is not simply the result of stress or difficult life circumstances. The key suicide risk factor is an undiagnosed, untreated, or ineffectively treated mental disorder. Research shows that over 90% of people who die by suicide have a mental disorder at the time of their death.

In teens, the mental disorders most closely linked to suicide risk are major depressive disorders, bipolar disorders, generalized anxiety disorders, conduct disorders, substance-use disorders, and eating disorders. While in some cases these disorders may be precipitated by environmental stressors, they can also occur as a result of changes in brain chemistry, even in the absence of an identifiable or obvious "reason."

Suicide is almost always complicated. In addition to the underlying disorders listed above, suicide risk can be affected by personality factors such as impulsivity, aggressiveness, and hopelessness. Moreover, suicide risk can be exacerbated by stressful life circumstances such as a history of childhood physical and/or sexual abuse; death, divorce, or other trauma in the family; persistent serious family conflict; traumatic breakups of romantic relationships; trouble with the law; academic failure and other major disappointments; and bullying, harassment, or victimization by peers.

It is important to remember that the vast majority of teens who experience even very stressful life events do *not* become suicidal. In some cases, such experiences can be a catalyst for suicidal behavior in teens who are already struggling with depression or other mental health problems. In other cases, traumatic experiences (such as prolonged bullying) can precipitate depression, anxiety, abuse of alcohol or drugs, or another mental disorder, which can increase suicide risk. Conversely, existing mental disorders may also lead to stressful life experiences such as family conflict, social isolation, relationship breakups, or academic failure, which may exacerbate the underlying illness and in turn increase suicide risk.

Warning Signs of Suicide

The signs listed below may mean someone is at risk for suicide. Risk is greater if a behavior is new or has recently increased in frequency or intensity, and if it seems related to a painful event, loss, or change.

- ☐ Talking about wanting to die or kill oneself
- ☐ Looking for ways to kill oneself, such as searching online or buying a gun
- ☐ Talking about feeling hopeless or having no reason to live
- ☐ Talking about feeling trapped or in unbearable pain
- ☐ Talking about being a burden to others
- ☐ Increasing the use of alcohol or drugs
- ☐ Acting anxious or agitated or behaving recklessly
- ☐ Sleeping too little or too much
- ☐ Withdrawing or feeling isolated
- ☐ Showing rage or talking about seeking revenge
- ☐ Displaying extreme mood swings

Tool 12: Relationship Between Suicide, Depression, Bullying, and NSSI

Depression: How Can We Help Students Identify Signs of Depression?

A promising addition to suicide prevention is depression screening. Before the development of depression screening programs, youth suicide-prevention programs only focused on training the adults to recognize warning signs of suicidal behavior in youth, and this was most often referred to as "gatekeeper training." The problem with providing suicide-prevention information only for school personnel and the other adults in the lives of students is that students are by far the most likely to share thoughts of suicide with their friends instead of the adults in their lives. Signs of Suicide (SOS), which is NREPP approved, is a questionnaire that students fill out asking questions about energy level, joy of life, and thoughts of suicide. Students score their own questionnaire and can determine if they are likely suffering from depression and need mental health services. Extensive information about SOS appears below. SOS is inexpensive, and the material has often been provided by SOS for free. Funding is available for SOS from the Montana DPHHS (contact Karl Rosston, the state suicide-prevention coordinator). The cost for the questionnaires and the ACT video is approximately $495.

SOS Signs of Suicide is a secondary-school-based suicide-prevention program that is listed as evidence-based in NREPP. The program includes screening and education. Students are screened for depression and suicide risk and referred for professional help as indicated. Students also view a video that teaches them to recognize signs of depression and suicide in themselves and others. They are taught that the appropriate response to these signs is to use the ACT technique: Acknowledge that there is a problem, let the person know you Care, and Tell a trusted adult. Students also participate in guided classroom discussions about suicide and depression. Research on the program has shown it reduces suicide attempts, increases knowledge about suicide and depression, and increases help-seeking behavior among middle school and high school students. In 2012, two additional gatekeeper tools were made available for use in program implementation: Training Trusted Adults, a 22-minute DVD for use in staff meetings or parent nights, and Plan, Prepare, Prevent: The SOS Online Gatekeeper Training, a 90-minute online course. A concern expressed by many educators is that if they implement the SOS program, many students will be identified as suicidal, and the school will not be able to follow up as needed with each student. The SOS website (www.mentalhealthscreening.org) provides many practical suggestions for overcoming resistance to screening and for implementation, and it recommends that only a manageable portion of the student body be screened at a time, so that follow-up and intervention can be provided.

Bullying and Suicide Prevention

School personnel have also asked about the relationship between bullying and suicide. Extensive research has found a strong association between bullying and suicide. Research has not identified causation between bullying and suicide as it is difficult to rule out the many other factors that involve family, possible abuse, mental illness, trauma, and loss. It is important to note that students who are depressed and anxious, have low self-esteem, and have few problem-solving skills are very likely to be the target of bullying. It is important for school personnel to know that there is a relationship between bullying and suicide. Children who have been bullied have reported a variety of behavioral, emotional, and social problems. With suicide being a leading cause of mortality in children and adolescents, it is troubling to note that studies reported positive associations between all bullying types and suicidal risks.

The following information about the connection between bully behaviors and the risk of suicidal ideation and attempt is critical:

- Both victims and perpetrators are at higher risk than peers, and a strong association exists between bullying and suicide.
- Personal characteristics such as internalizing problems, low self-esteem, and low assertiveness increase the risk of being bullied, and these factors are also associated with suicide risk.
- It is difficult to control all the risk factors to determine if being bullied was a proximal cause to a youth suicide.
- LGBTQ youth have higher rates of suicide attempts and deaths than their heterosexual peers, but "there is nothing inherently suicidal about same-sex orientation." It is the result of external factors such as bullying, harassment, abuse, rejection, and lack of support. The strongest protective factor is parental acceptance.

Montana school personnel who know a student is involved in bullying should not hesitate to ask the student about hopelessness and thoughts of suicide.

Additional information and resources about bullying and suicide can be found at www.sprc.org/sites/sprc.org/files/library/Suicide_Bullying_Issue_Brief.pdf

Suicide and Non-Suicidal Self-Injury

NSSI (non-suicidal self-injury) is a behavior that has caught school personnel by surprise with the frequency of incidents and the complexity of the behavior. The behavior is most common in adolescents but has also increased with upper-elementary-aged students. This section will answer the following questions:

- What exactly is non-suicidal self-injury?
- How many students engage in it?
- Why do adolescents engage in it?
- What is the school's role with NSSI?
- Do parents need to be notified?
- What is the relationship between NSSI and suicide?
- What is the best treatment for NSSI?

NSSI is defined as the purposeful harming of one's body with suicidal intent. The most common forms are cutting, burning, scratching of the skin, or not letting wounds heal. This behavior fulfills a multitude of complex needs for the student engaging in it, and it is often addictive. The most common theories for NSSI are the following:

- The act has a biological basis as endorphins are released (much like those released during exercise).
- The act provides a psychological regulation of emotions as students concentrate on the injury and are able to shut out the conflict they are having at the moment (such as an argument with their parent(s) or a peer or a disappointment in their life).
- The most common motivation for this behavior is to release endorphins (many who engage in NSSI regularly have described it as addictive) or to regulate emotion by concentrating on the injury and bleeding rather than the precipitating event, such as an argument or disappointment.

More information is available from Cornell in the handout entitled *What is Self-Injury?* available at www.selfinjury.bctr.cornell.edu/.

NSSI is a highly preventative and episodic behavior for adolescents with some studies estimating that as many as 18% of adolescents report engaging in this behavior at least once. Research indicates that 6% to 8% of adolescents engage in the behavior repetitively, and that more girls engage in it than boys. A common denominator found with students who self-injure is a trauma history of loss or abuse. Most young people engaging in NSSI are cleverly hiding the behavior from adults. The most common parts of the body that are injured are the arms, thighs, and stomach. Students often wear long-sleeved shirts or sweaters, even in the summer, or wear many bracelets to hide the signs of NSSI. NSSI is also associated with mental illness such as anxiety, depression, and borderline personality disorder.

School personnel need to know the incidence of NSSI and be alert to the warning signs (such as frequent or unexplained bruises, scars, cuts, or burns) and the wearing of inappropriate clothing designed to conceal wounds. Secretive behaviors such as spending unusual amounts of time in the school bathrooms or isolated areas on campus may also be a warning sign. Students might show evidence of the behavior in work samples, journals, or art projects. Students might also be in possession of sharp instruments such as razor blades, shards of glass, or thumb tacks.

Schools need to develop a protocol to respond to a student engaging in NSSI, and it is recommended that the school counselor and school nurse be involved. A staff member who suspects the behavior should approach the student in a confidential manner or go with the student to see a counselor or nurse. A typical adult response to NSSI is to be horrified and demand that the student stops engaging in the behavior. It is not that simple. The behavior is complex and is working to help the student cope with the issues in their life. Educators need to respond with compassion and empathy and recognize the struggle the student is experiencing. The focus should be on the underlying issues the student is experiencing. Helping the student gain control over NSSI and diminish the behavior is the goal.

Interventions with NSSI need to be done individually, and school counselors and nurses can help students learn substitute behaviors that will distract the student when they are having the urge to cut or burn their skin. These substitute behaviors are things like scratching clothing, standing on tiptoe, scribbling with a red marker, tearing paper, or playing with play-dough. Extensive information about substitute behaviors and distraction techniques is available from Cornell in a handout entitled Distraction Techniques and Alternative Coping Strategies and can be found at www.selfinjury.bctr.cornell.edu.

In addition, school counselors and nurses can help students keep a trigger log of the antecedents and situations that caused them to want to self-injure and can explore with them better ways to manage the situation.

Parent notification when a student is known to be engaging in NSSI has been a controversial issue. The counseling/psychology literature has been inconsistent with those who caution against parent notification concerned about loss of rapport with the student. There has been one legal case in New Jersey where the school system and the counselor were sued over the issue of parent notification of an adolescent girl engaging in NSSI. The counselor who was taken to court maintained that the parent was notified of the concern about NSSI for her child. The parent maintained that school personnel knew about the behavior but never contacted her. The counselor had no record of the parent notification. The school counselor was not found liable. One of the authors of this report was an expert witness in the case.

It is highly recommended that parents be notified by school personnel when a student is engaging in NSSI. The ideal notification would be a conference with key school personnel, parents, and the student, who should be given the opportunity of explaining/discussing the NSSI behaviors. School personnel should follow the parent notification procedures and referral procedures that are outlined in this toolkit for notification of suicidal behavior. A referral needs to be made for the student to receive treatment in the community. This toolkit emphasized that when a student is believed to be suicidal, and parents are not receptive to obtaining community mental health interventions for their child, the state protective services need to be notified. If parents are not receptive to obtaining outside services for their child engaging in NSSI, things are not as clear because the student is not in imminent danger. Each school district will have to decide what their protocol is in this situation, but follow-up and support services for the student are essential whether outside mental health services are obtained or not.

What is the relationship between suicide and NSSI? School personnel may think that the two behaviors are exclusive. However, NSSI has been added as a risk factor for suicide because students engaging in NSSI are becoming comfortable with the habit of harming their body. Research estimates are that approximately 30% of adolescents who repetitively self-injure ultimately make a suicide attempt. The NSSI risk factors for suicide are the following:

- Utilizing multiple methods
- Having a long-standing history of NSSI
- Reporting little physical pain from NSSI
- Reporting disassociation when engaging in NSSI

School personnel should not hesitate to ask a student known to be engaging in self-injury about thoughts of suicide, and parental notification procedures need to be followed and referrals made to community providers skilled in managing NSSI. If the student admits to suicidal thoughts, safety planning and pathways to care procedures for suicide outlined in this toolkit must be followed. A video on NSSI created by Dr. Scott Poland for the state of Florida provided critical insight into self-injury as he interviewed two young women who received a national award for their willingness to discuss their struggle with self-injury. The video is available free of charge at www.nova.edu/suicideprevention
(under Training Videos).

Tool 13: Parental Involvement in Suicide Prevention

How can Montana schools increase parental involvement and awareness of youth suicide?

Part 2 of this Toolkit outlines practical steps for schools to follow for parent notification and for referral to community-based services when a student is suspected of being suicidal

Appendix 1 provides answers to the most frequently asked questions by parents about suicide prevention and mental health.

Tool 29 provides an overview of information about suicide prevention that is recommended to be posted on every school district website in Montana. It outlines warning signs, crisis helpline numbers, and, most importantly, who to contact at your child's school if you believe your child is suicidal.

Since suicide is the second leading cause of death for children and adolescents in Montana, schools are encouraged to include warning signs of depression in a variety of presentations to parents. For example, if a program is provided for parents on the high school graduation plan, a few minutes should be set aside to outline key warning signs of suicide. Epidemiology studies done by the Center for Disease Control in the aftermath of youth suicide clusters have found that parents were slow to recognize the mental illness of their child and did not obtain the needed treatment. Parents need to know that suicide is almost always the result of untreated or undertreated mental illness, and that evidence-based treatments exist for all mental illnesses. Parents of adolescents in particular may think that their child's moodiness and irritability are typical of being a teen, but three questions need to be considered:

1. Has this behavior gone on for several weeks or more (persistent)?
2. Is the behavior affecting all aspects of their life, school, friends, and family (pervasive)?
3. Have they dropped out of previously enjoyed activities? For example, she did not want to be on the dance team this year, but she has done it for years and really enjoyed it.

Additionally, schools are encouraged to provide developmentally appropriate presentations regularly for parents of children of all ages that emphasize the following:

- being involved in their child's life
- knowing their friends and the friends' parents
- knowing signs of anxiety and depression
- separating their misbehavior from their worth as a person
- recognizing technology is a privilege and not a right
- ensuring technology-free times in their homes
- regularly eating meals as a family
- modeling coping during difficult times
- avoiding putting children in the middle of a divorce
- knowing the importance of both parents staying involved in their child's life regardless of the circumstances of separation or divorce.

Parents are encouraged to have deep conversations with their children about what is going on in their lives and to be careful not to question too much but to focus on listening. Parents who have any reason to think their child might be suicidal are encouraged to *ask*. Dr. Scott Poland has a PowerPoint presentation for parents of children of all ages: Parenting in a Challenging World. It can be emailed to school personnel in Montana upon request. He can be contacted at spoland@nova.edu.

Suicide-Prevention Videos Specifically for Parents:

Society for the Prevention of Teen Suicide (www.sptsusa.org/) has an 18-minute video for parents: Not My Kid. It is available for free at www.sptsusa.org/not-my-kid/.

Montana DPHHS (dphhs.mt.gov/amdd/suicide) has a 4-minute video for parents describing the warning signs. It is produced by the Mayo Clinic and can be accessed at

www.youtube.com/watch?v=3BByqa7bhto&feature=youtu.be.

Tool 14A: C-SSRS Brief Screening

Suicide Ideation: Definitions and Prompts		
	Past Month	
Ask questions that are in bold. Begin with questions 1 and 2.	**YES**	**NO**
1) Wish to Be Dead: Person endorses thoughts about a wish to be dead or not alive anymore, or a wish to fall asleep and not wake up. **Have you wished you were dead or wished you could go to sleep and not wake up?**		
2) Suicidal Thoughts: General non-specific thoughts of wanting to end one's life/die by suicide, "I've thought about killing myself," without general thoughts of ways to kill oneself/associated methods, intent, or plan. **Have you actually had any thoughts of killing yourself?**		
If YES to 2, ask questions 3, 4, 5, and 6. If NO to 2, go directly to question 6.		
3) Suicidal Thoughts with Method (Without Specific Plan or Intent to Act): Person endorses thoughts of suicide and has thought of a least one method during the assessment period. This is different than a specific plan with time, place, or method details worked out. "I thought about taking an overdose, but I never made a specific plan as to when, where, or how I would actually do it….and I would never go through with it." **Have you been thinking about how you might do this?**		
4) Suicidal Intent (Without Specific Plan): Active suicidal thoughts of killing oneself, and patient reports having *some intent to act on such thoughts*, as opposed to "I have the thoughts, but I definitely will not do anything about them." **Have you had these thoughts and had some intention of acting on them?**		
5) Suicide Intent with Specific Plan: Thoughts of killing oneself with details of plan fully or partially worked out, and person has some intent to carry it out. **Have you started to work out or worked out the details of how to kill yourself? Do you intend to carry out this plan?**		
6) Suicide Behavior Question:	**Lifetime**	
Have you ever done anything, started to do anything, or prepared to do anything to end your life?		
Examples: Collected pills, obtained a gun, gave away valuables, wrote a will or suicide note, took out pills but didn't swallow any, held a gun but changed your mind or it was grabbed from your hand, went to the roof but didn't jump; or actually took pills, tried to shoot yourself, cut yourself, tried to hang yourself, etc.	**Past 3 Months**	
If YES, ask: Were any of these in the past 3 months?		

☐ Low Risk   ☐ Moderate Risk   ■ High Risk

For inquiries and training information, contact: Kelly Posner, PhD. New York State Psychiatric Institute, 1051 Riverside Drive, New York, New York, 10032; posnerk@nyspi.columbia.edu

Tool 14B: SAFE-T Protocol with C-SSRS - Recent

Step 1: Identify Risk Factors	
C-SSRS Suicidal Ideation Severity	**Month**
1) Wish to Be Dead: **Have you wished you were dead or wished you could go to sleep and not wake up?**	
2) Current Suicidal Thoughts: **Have you actually had any thoughts of killing yourself?**	
3) Suicidal Thoughts with Method **(Without Specific Plan or Intent to Act)**: **Have you been thinking about how you might do this?**	
4) Suicidal Intent (Without Specific Plan): **Have you had these thoughts and had some intention of acting on them?**	
5) Intent with Plan: **Have you started to work out or worked out the details of how to kill yourself? Do you intend to carry out this plan?**	
C-SSRS Suicidal Behavior **Have you ever done anything, started to do anything, or prepared to do anything to end your life?** Examples: Collected pills, obtained a gun, gave away valuables, wrote a will or suicide note, took out pills but didn't swallow any, held a gun but changed your mind or it was grabbed from your hand, went to the roof but didn't jump; or actually took pills, tried to shoot yourself, cut yourself, tried to hang yourself, etc. **If "YES" Was it within the past 3 months?**	**Lifetime** **Past 3 Months**

Current and Past Psychiatric Diagnoses:

- ☐ Mood disorder
- ☐ Psychotic disorder
- ☐ Alcohol-/substance-abuse disorders
- ☐ PTSD
- ☐ ADHD
- ☐ TBI
- ☐ Cluster B personality disorders or traits
  (i.e., borderline, antisocial, histrionic, and narcissistic)
- ☐ Conduct problems (antisocial behavior, aggression, impulsivity)
- ☐ Recent onset

Presenting Symptoms:

- ☐ Anhedonia
- ☐ Impulsivity
- ☐ Hopelessness or despair
- ☐ Anxiety and/or panic
- ☐ Insomnia
- ☐ Command hallucinations
- ☐ Psychosis

Family History:

- ☐ Suicide
- ☐ Suicidal behavior
- ☐ Axis I psychiatric diagnoses requiring hospitalization

Precipitants/Stressors:

- ☐ Triggering events leading to humiliation, shame, and/or despair (e.g., loss of relationship, financial, or health status) (real or anticipated)
- ☐ Chronic physical pain or other acute medical problem (e.g., CNS disorders)
- ☐ Sexual/physical abuse
- ☐ Substance intoxication or withdrawal
- ☐ Pending incarceration or homelessness
- ☐ Legal problems
- ☐ Inadequate social supports
- ☐ Social isolation
- ☐ Perceived burden on others

Change in treatment:

- ☐ Recent inpatient discharge
- ☐ Change in provider or treatment (i.e., medications, psychotherapy, milieu)
- ☐ Hopeless or dissatisfied with provider or treatment
- ☐ Noncompliant or not receiving treatment

☐ **Access to lethal methods: Ask _specifically_ about presence or absence of a firearm in the home or ease of accessing a firearm.**

Step 2: Identify Protective Factors

(Protective factors may not counteract significant acute suicide risk factors)

Internal:
□ Ability to cope with stress
□ Frustration tolerance
□ Religious beliefs
□ Fear of death or the actual act of killing oneself
□ Identifies reasons for living

External:
□ Cultural, spiritual, and/or moral attitudes against suicide
□ Responsibility to children
□ Beloved pets
□ Supportive social network of family or friends
□ Positive therapeutic relationships
□ Engaged in work or school

Step 3: Specific Questioning About Thoughts, Plans, and Suicidal Intent

(see Step 1 for Ideation Severity and Behavior)

If semi-structured interview is preferred to complete this section, clinicians may opt to complete C-SSRS Lifetime/Recent for comprehensive behavior/lethality assessment.

C-SSRS Suicidal Ideation Intensity (with respect to the most severe ideation 1–5 identified above)	Month
Frequency: **How many times have you had these thoughts?** (1) Less than once a week (2) Once a week (3) 2–5 times a week (4) Daily or almost daily (5) Many times each day	
Duration: **When you have the thoughts, how long do they last?** (1) Fleeting—a few seconds or minutes (4) 4–8 hours/most of the day (2) Less than 1 hour/some of the time (5) More than 8 hours/persistent or continuous (3) 1–4 hours/a lot of the time	
Controllability: **Could/can you stop thinking about killing yourself or wanting to die if you want to?** (1) Easily able to control thoughts (4) Can control thoughts with a lot of difficulty (2) Can control thoughts with little difficulty (5) Unable to control thoughts (3) Can control thoughts with some difficulty (0) Does not attempt to control thoughts	
Deterrents: **Are there things—anyone or anything (e.g., family, religion, pain of death)—that stopped you from wanting to die or acting on thoughts of suicide?** (1) Deterrents definitely stopped you from attempting suicide (4) Deterrents most likely did not stop you (2) Deterrents probably stopped you (5) Deterrents definitely did not stop you (3) Uncertain that deterrents stopped you (0) Does not apply	
Reasons for Ideation: **What sort of reasons did you have for thinking about wanting to die or killing yourself? Was it to end the pain or stop the way you were feeling (in other words, you couldn't go on living with this pain or how you were feeling), or was it to get attention, revenge, or a reaction from others? Or both?** (1) Completely to get attention, revenge, or a reaction from others (4) Mostly to end or stop the pain (you couldn't go on living with the pain or how you were feeling) (2) Mostly to get attention, revenge, or a reaction from others (3) Equally to get attention, revenge, or a reaction from others and to end/stop the pain (5) Completely to end or stop the pain (you couldn't go on living with the pain or how you were feeling) (0) Does not apply	
Total Score:	

Step 4: Guidelines to Determine Risk Level and Develop Interventions to LOWER Risk Level

"The estimation of suicide risk, at the culmination of the suicide assessment, is the quintessential *clinical judgment*, since no study has identified one specific risk factor or set of risk factors as specifically predictive of suicide or other suicidal behavior."

From The American Psychiatric Association,
Practice Guidelines for the Assessment and Treatment of Patients with Suicidal Behaviors.

Risk Stratification	Triage
High Suicide Risk ☐ Suicidal ideation with intent or intent with plan **in the past month** (C-SSRS Suicidal Ideation #4 or #5) Or ☐ Suicidal behavior **within the past 3 months** (C-SSRS Suicidal Behavior)	✈ Initiate local psychiatric admission process ✈ Stay with patient until transfer to higher level of care is complete ✈ Follow-up and document outcome of emergency psychiatric evaluation
Moderate Suicide Risk ☐ Suicidal ideation with method, **without plan, intent, or behavior in the past month** (C-SSRS Suicidal Ideation #3) Or ☐ Suicidal behavior more than 3 months ago (C-SSRS Suicidal Behavior Lifetime) Or ☐ Multiple risk factors and few protective factors	✈ Directly address suicide risk, implementing suicide- prevention strategies ✈ Develop Safety Plan
Low Suicide Risk ☐ Wish to die or Suicidal Ideation **without method, intent, plan, or behavior** (C-SSRS Suicidal Ideation #1 or #2) Or ☐ Modifiable risk factors and strong protective factors Or ☐ No reported history of Suicidal Ideation or Behavior	✈ Discretionary outpatient referral

Step 5: Documentation

Risk Level: ☐ **High Suicide Risk**   ☐ **Moderate Suicide Risk**   ☐ **Low Suicide Risk**

Clinical Notes:

☐ Your clinical observations
☐ Relevant mental status information
☐ Methods of suicide risk evaluation

☐ Brief evaluation summary
    ☐ Warning signs
    ☐ Risk indicators
    ☐ Protective factors
    ☐ Access to lethal means
    ☐ Collateral sources used and relevant information obtained
    ☐ Specific assessment data to support risk determination
    ☐ Rationale for actions taken and not taken

☐ Provision of Crisis Line 1-800-273-TALK (8255)
☐ Implementation of Safety Plan (if applicable)

Tool 15A: Suicide Risk Monitoring Tool—Elementary/Middle School

Student's Name: _____	**Date:** _____
Completed by: _____	**Title:** _____

I. IDEATION

Are you having thoughts of suicide?	☐ Yes ☐ No
Right now	☐ Yes ☐ No
Past 24 hours	☐ Yes ☐ No
Past week	☐ Yes ☐ No
Past month	☐ Yes ☐ No
How often do you have these thoughts? (Frequency)	☐ Less than weekly ☐ weekly ☐ daily ☐ hourly ☐ every minute
How long do these thoughts last? (Duration)	☐ A few seconds ☐ minutes ☐ hours ☐ days ☐ weeks or more
How disruptive are these thoughts to your life? (Intensity)	☐ not at all ☐ somewhat ☐ a great deal

II. INTENT

How much do you want to die?	☐ not at all ☐ somewhat ☐ a great deal
How much do you want to live?	☐ not at all ☐ somewhat ☐ a great deal

III. PLAN

Do you have a plan?	☐ Yes ☐ No
Have you written a suicide note?	☐ Yes ☐ No
Have you identified a method?	☐ Yes ☐ No
Do you have access to the method?	☐ Yes ☐ No ☐ N/A
Have you identified when and where you would carry out this plan?	☐ Yes ☐ No ☐ N/A
Have you made a recent attempt?	☐ Yes ☐ No
If so, when / how / where?	_____

IV. WARNING SIGNS

How hopeless do you feel that things will get better?	☐ not at all ☐ somewhat ☐ a great deal
How much do you feel like a burden to others?	☐ not at all ☐ somewhat ☐ a great deal
How depressed, sad, or down do you currently feel?	☐ not at all ☐ somewhat ☐ a great deal
How disconnected do you feel from others?	☐ not at all ☐ somewhat ☐ a great deal
Is there a particular trigger/stressor for this student?	☐ Yes ☐ No
If so, what?	_____
Has it improved?	☐ not at all ☐ somewhat ☐ a great deal

V. PROTECTIVE FACTORS

Reasons for Living	**Supportive People**
(things good at / like to do / enjoy / other)	(family / adults/ friends / peers)
What could change about your life that would make you no longer want to die?	

FOR THE CLINICIAN—SUMMARY PAGE

Elementary school / middle school students

This is meant as a screening tool for suicide risk management. It is not a comprehensive measure for suicide risk assessment. At times, we must monitor ongoing suicidality of students who have already been assessed either by you, an outside mental health professional, or in a hospital setting. Clinicians working with suicidal students often report being unsure when a student may need re-hospitalization or further intervention, and when levels of suicidality are remaining relatively stable for that *individual* student. Monitoring suicidality and managing risk over time are the purposes of this form.

We have created two versions of this tool as elementary and early middle school students are better able to identify responses when provided with less choices than older middle school and high school students. With elementary and early middle school students, the clinician should complete this form through collaborative discussion with the child during each session or meeting. Alter the wording as needed to make it developmentally appropriate to ensure the child understands what you are asking.

As you know your student best, we have created within this form a place to document the particular triggers or stressors for this individual. This will allow you to monitor and track their unique stressors over time.

VI. CURRENT RISK LEVEL

Recommendations for further treatment and management of suicide risk should be a direct result of the ratings of risk as identified below in collaboration with your school district procedure. In all cases, parents should be notified to inform them you met with their child.

Student meets criteria for low/moderate/high suicide risk based on the following information (If a student falls between levels, err on the side of caution and assume the higher risk category):

- ☐ Low risk: No or passing ideation that does not interfere with activities of daily living; reports no desire to die (i.e., intent), has no specific plan, exhibits few risk factors, has identifiable protective factors.
- ☐ Moderate risk: Reports frequent suicidal ideation with limited intensity and duration; has some specific plans to die by suicide but no reported intent; demonstrates some risk factors but is able to identify reasons for living and other protective factors. Students who have a previous history of a suicide attempt will remain at least at the moderate risk level.
- ☐ High risk: Reports frequent, intense, and enduring suicidal ideation; has written suicide note or reports specific plans, including choice of lethal methods and availability/accessibility of the method. Student presents with multiple risk factors and identifies few if any protective factors.

VII. ACTIONS TAKEN / RECOMMENDATIONS

Parent/guardian contacted?	☐ Yes ☐ No
Released to parent/guardian?	☐ Yes ☐ No
Referrals provided to parent?	☐ Yes ☐ No
Safety Plan developed?	☐ Yes ☐ No
Recommending removal of method/means?	☐ Yes ☐ No
If currently in treatment, contact made with therapist/psychiatrist?	☐ Yes ☐ No
Outpatient therapy recommended?	☐ Yes ☐ No
Recommending 24-hour supervision?	☐ Yes ☐ No
Hospitalization recommended?	☐ Yes ☐ No
Other? Please describe:	_____

Tool 15B: Suicide Risk Monitoring Tool—Middle School/High School

Student's Name: _____	Date: _____
Completed by: _____	Title: _____

I. IDEATION

Are you having thoughts of suicide?	☐ Yes ☐ No
Right now	☐ Yes ☐ No
Past 24 hours	☐ Yes ☐ No
Past week	☐ Yes ☐ No
Past month	☐ Yes ☐ No
How often do you have these thoughts? (Frequency)	☐ Less than weekly ☐ weekly ☐ daily ☐ hourly ☐ every minute
How long do these thoughts last? (Duration)	☐ A few seconds ☐ minutes ☐ hours ☐ days ☐ a week or more
How disruptive are these thoughts to your life? (Intensity)	not at all= 1 ☐ 2 ☐ 3 ☐ 4 ☐ 5 ☐ =a great deal

II. INTENT

How much do you want to die?	not at all= 1 ☐ 2 ☐ 3 ☐ 4 ☐ 5 ☐ =a great deal
How much do you want to live?	not at all= 1 ☐ 2 ☐ 3 ☐ 4 ☐ 5 ☐ =a great deal

III. PLAN

Do you have a plan?	☐ Yes ☐ No
Have you written a suicide note?	☐ Yes ☐ No
Have you identified a method?	☐ Yes ☐ No
Do you have access to the method?	☐ Yes ☐ No ☐ N/A
Have you identified when and where you would carry out this plan?	☐ Yes ☐ No ☐ N/A
Have you made a recent attempt?	☐ Yes ☐ No
If so, when / how / where?	_____

IV. WARNING SIGNS

How hopeless do you feel that things will get better?	not at all= 1 ☐ 2 ☐ 3 ☐ 4 ☐ 5 ☐ =a great deal
How much do you feel like a burden to others?	not at all= 1 ☐ 2 ☐ 3 ☐ 4 ☐ 5 ☐ =a great deal
How depressed, sad, or down do you currently feel?	not at all= 1 ☐ 2 ☐ 3 ☐ 4 ☐ 5 ☐ =a great deal
How disconnected do you feel from others?	not at all= 1 ☐ 2 ☐ 3 ☐ 4 ☐ 5 ☐ =a great deal
Is there a particular trigger/stressor for this student?	☐ Yes ☐ No
If so, what?	_____
Has it improved?	not at all= 1 ☐ 2 ☐ 3 ☐ 4 ☐ 5 ☐ =a great deal

V. PROTECTIVE FACTORS

Reasons for Living	**Supportive People**
(things good at / like to do / enjoy / other)	(family / adults/ friends / peers)
What could change about your life that would make you no longer want to die?	

FOR THE CLINICIAN—SUMMARY PAGE

Middle school / High school students

This is meant as a screening tool for suicide risk management. It is not a comprehensive measure for suicide risk assessment. At times, we must monitor ongoing suicidality of students who have already been assessed either by you, an outside mental health professional, or in a hospital setting. Clinicians working with suicidal students often report being unsure when a student may need re-hospitalization or further intervention, and when levels of suicidality are remaining relatively stable for that *individual* student. Monitoring suicidality and managing risk over time are the purposes of this form.

We have created two versions of this tool as older middle school and high school students are better able to identify responses when provided with more choices than elementary and early middle school students. With older middle school and high school students, complete this form with them the first time, explaining each area and ensuring they understand how to complete it. During subsequent sessions, they can complete the form independently, followed by a collaborative discussion of risk and treatment planning.

As you know your student best, we have created within this form a place to document the particular triggers or stressors for this individual. This will allow you to monitor and track their unique stressors over time.

VI. CURRENT RISK LEVEL

Recommendations for further treatment and management of suicide risk should be a direct result of the ratings of risk as identified below in collaboration with your school district procedure. In all cases, parents should be notified to inform them you met with their child.

Student meets criteria for low/moderate/high suicide risk based on the following information (If a student falls between levels, err on the side of caution and assume the higher risk category):

- Low risk: No or passing ideation that does not interfere with activities of daily living; reports no desire to die (i.e., intent), has no specific plan, exhibits few risk factors, has identifiable protective factors.
- Moderate risk: Reports frequent suicidal ideation with limited intensity and duration; has some specific plans to die by suicide but no reported intent; demonstrates some risk factors but is able to identify reasons for living and other protective factors. Students who have a previous history of a suicide attempt will remain at least at the moderate risk level.
- High risk: Reports frequent, intense, and enduring suicidal ideation; has written suicide note or reports specific plans, including choice of lethal methods and availability/accessibility of the method. Student presents with multiple risk factors and identifies few if any protective factors.

VII. ACTIONS TAKEN / RECOMMENDATIONS

Parent/guardian contacted?	☐ Yes	☐ No
Released to parent/guardian?	☐ Yes	☐ No
Referrals provided to parent?	☐ Yes	☐ No
Safety Plan developed?	☐ Yes	☐ No
Recommending removal of method/means?	☐ Yes	☐ No
If currently in treatment, contact made with therapist/psychiatrist?	☐ Yes	☐ No
Outpatient therapy recommended?	☐ Yes	☐ No
Recommending 24-hour supervision?	☐ Yes	☐ No
Hospitalization recommended?	☐ Yes	☐ No
Other? Please describe:	_____	

Tool 16: Suicide Risk Report

Student Suicide Risk Report

Assessed Risk Level: ☐ Low   ☐ Medium   ☐ High

Student:	Date:
Counselor/Suicide-Response Designee:	School:
Administrator:	Grade:
Risk Assessment Completed by:	Notification of Student's Counselor: ☐ Yes ☐ No

Actions Taken

Date	Action	Members Present	Notes
	Student Conference		
	Notified Principal and Key Personnel		
	Parent Contacted		
	Parent Conference		
	Student Safety Plan		
	Parent Acknowledgement Form Signed		
	Release of Information Signed		
	Mental Health Care Provider Referral		
	Other Community Referral(s)		

Follow-Up Documentation

Student:

Parent:

Community Resource:

Copy for student's counselor, suicide-response designee, and designated administrator

Tool 17: Safety Plan

Safety Plan		
Student:	School Caregiver:	Date:
Step 1: Warning signs (thoughts, images, mood, situation, behavior) that a suicidal crisis may be developing		
1. 2. 3.		
Step 2: How can I keep myself safe? How can I keep my environment safe?		
1. 2. 3. 4. The one thing that is most important to me and worth living for is: _____		
Step 3: Trusted adults at school, at home, or in my community whom I can ask for help		
1. Name: 2. Name: 3. Name:		Phone: Phone: Phone:
Step 4: Internal coping strategies—thins I can do to take my mind off my problems without contacting another person (relaxation techniques, physical activities)		
1. 2.		
Step 5: Professionals or agencies I can contact during a crisis		
Clinician name:	Phone:	Pager/emergency contact number:
Local urgent care services:	Phone:	Address:
Step 6: Making the environment safe		
1. 2.		
Suicide-Prevention Lifeline Phone: 1-800-273-TALK (8255) CrisisTextLine.org (24 hours, nationwide): text "start" or "help" to 741741 Have an iPhone? Talk to Siri for connection to help.		
Student signature:		Staff signature:
Adapted from Stanley, B. & Brown, G.K. (2011). Safety Planning Intervention: A Brief Intervention to Mitigate Suicide Risk. *Cognitive and Behavioral Practice*. 19, 256–264		

Tool 18: Parent Acknowledgement Form for Student at Risk of Suicide (sample)

Parent Acknowledgement Form for Student at Risk of Suicide

School:	Student:	Date:

As the parent/guardian of the student whose name is _____, I have authority to make decisions on behalf of the student and have the authority to sign this document. I acknowledge that I have been advised by school staff member _____on _____(date) that my child has expressed suicidal ideation and may be at risk of suicide.

I understand that I have been advised to immediately take my child to the appropriate medical and/or mental health providers for evaluation and any treatment recommended by the provider.

I agree to provide appropriate information to _____(name of school staff member) regarding any evaluations and/or treatment received from the mental health provider that will prepare the school to support the student's reentry into the academic setting.

_____(name of staff member) will follow up with me and the student within one week from the date of this letter as well as other times that the staff member determines.

I understand that any referral information provided to me that identifies medical, mental health, or related health providers is meant for my consideration only, and it is not a requirement that I use these providers. I am free to select other providers of my choice.

The school/district is not responsible for evaluation expenses for any service providers.

Parent/Guardian Information

Name:	
Address:	Date:
Phone:	Parent/guardian signature:
Copies provided for parent/guardian, suicide-response designee, administrative designee	Date:
	Staff member signature:

Tool 19: The Parent Conference

The Parent Conference
1) Begin by asking parents how their child has been doing, and if they have noted any changes in their child's behavior.
2) State what you have noticed in their child's behavior and ask how that fits with what they have seen in their child.
3) Advise parents to remove lethal means from the home as their child is possibly suicidal. You can equate this to how you would advise taking car keys from a youth who had been drinking. Montana has a higher rate of youth suicide deaths by firearms than the national averages, and several initiatives for storage of firearms away from young people and recognizing removing lethal means from the ready access of a suicidal individuals are available at www.dphhs.mt.gov/amdd/suicide. Fourteen states and the District of Columbia have laws imposing criminal liability when a child gains access as a result of negligent storage of a firearm. Typically, these laws apply whenever the person "knows or reasonably should know" that a child is likely to gain access to the firearm. Montana is not one of those states. However, Montana OPI's website (opi.mt.gov/) provides important information for prevention. Key school personnel such as counselors and/or suicide-prevention experts are encouraged to ask students directly about their child's access to a gun and to recommend strongly to parents that guns be safely stored.
4) Acknowledge the emotional state of the parents. Provide empathy for this situation and comment on its scary nature for parents.
5) Acknowledge that it is essential for schools, parents, and community mental health and medical services to collaborate to help a suicidal child as no one can do this alone.
6) If the parent appears to be uncooperative or unwilling to take certain actions, find out their beliefs about youth suicide risk/behavior and see if there are myths they believe that are blocking them from taking proper action.
7) Acknowledge and explore any cultural, religious, or other concerns that might reduce the parent's acceptance of mental health treatment for their child.
8) When possible, align yourself with the parent. It is important for them to understand the stress and depression their child is likely experiencing and to discuss with the parents ways to alleviate stress and how to obtain mental health assistance for their child.
9) Refer parents to local community mental health treatment that the school has previously worked well with and explain what parents can expect from the treatment of their child. (Key questions that referring school personnel can ask community services providers to determine their competence in suicide assessment and management are outlined in Section 2 and in Tool 28.)
10) Clarify the role of the school and the follow-up that will be done at school.
11) Persuasively request that parents sign a release of information form so that designated school personnel can speak directly with community mental health professionals. State clearly that you will be checking with the student and their parents to verify that community-based mental health services were obtained.

12) Document all actions that include having parents sign an emergency notification or parent acknowledgment of suicidal concern form (Tool 18). If parents refuse to sign the notification form, ask another staff member to witness their refusal.

13) If parents ask that their child be allowed to walk home, ride the bus, or drive themselves home, insist that they come to school and pick up their child.

14) It is also anticipated that parents might be difficult to reach, and school personnel should keep the student suspected of being suicidal under close supervision until they can be transferred to their parents. If parents simply cannot be reached, school personnel need to work with local law enforcement and/or mental health personnel to secure the needed supervision for the student.

15) Suicide risk will fluctuate, especially with school-age students, and it is very important for school personnel and community providers to monitor suicide risk with students who are known to have been suicidal. Suicide Risk Monitoring Tools are available (Tool 15A for elementary school/middle school students and Tool 15B for middle school/high school students.

Tool 20: Checklist for School Reentry of Suicidal Student

Principal or Designee

- ☐ Meet with student's parent(s)/guardian(s) to discuss reentry and steps needed to ensure the student has a successful return to school.
- ☐ Review student's progress with mental health provider outside of school as hopefully the Release of Information form has been signed. If it has not, discuss with parents/guardians and persuade them of the necessity and benefits for their child if this communication is allowed.
- ☐ Review all information from the mental health provider, especially with regards to safety planning and needed support services at school.
- ☐ Plan the follow-up services within the school community that will be available to the parents/guardians and the student.
- ☐ Discuss any foreseeable social and/or academic challenges their child will experience and make a plan for easing those challenges.

Counselor or Designated Staff Member
(such as Suicide Prevention/Risk Specialist)

- ☐ Meet with the student on first day of return before he/she attends any classes. Regularly check in with the student to assess his/her adjustment to academic and social environment (minimum weekly is recommended).
- ☐ Discuss with student the progress he/she feels they made while under mental health care.
  - o Do they feel hopeful for the future?
  - o Are they looking forward to getting back to classes?
  - o Are they looking forward to meeting up with friends?
  - o Who are their friends?
- ☐ Help them identify and know how to find you (or another adult they express trust in) if they are distressed or have a question.
- ☐ Review the plan for staying in touch with him/her to make sure they are adjusting to the academic and social requirements.
- ☐ If the student has been out for an extended time, missed assignments may have to be prioritized by importance and counselor coordination with teachers is advised in order to set up a manageable schedule for the student. Also, consider postponing interim or final course grades until the student has had time to catch up.
- ☐ Provide appropriate information to the student's teachers and any other staff on a need-to-know basis, so they can be alert to any further warning signs.

Tool 21: Checklist for Postvention Steps After a Suicide

Principal
☐ Contact the police to confirm the death and the facts surrounding it.
☐ Notify district superintendent or suicide-prevention designee.
☐ Call neighboring schools for extra counseling support for students and staff; for example, the elementary school or middle school the deceased attended and/or the high school the deceased was scheduled to attend.
☐ Activate phone tree, including Crisis Response Team, school staff, transportation administrator (if student rode the bus), and coach (if student was an athlete). Notify other school principals that may be impacted where siblings of deceased or friends of deceased attend.
☐ Contact family of deceased student in person to offer condolences and assistance. Obtain permission from parent to release cause of death. Respect wishes if they refuse to provide information.
☐ Schedule a faculty meeting as soon as possible: before school if incident happened the day before, or at the end of school in preparation for the next day if notification of incident came during the school day.
o Dispel rumors by providing only the facts.
o Allow staff to ask questions and express feelings.
o Review process for students who want to leave the campus due to the incident.
o Remind staff to not speak to media and provide them with a prepared statement that can be used for any unexpected calls from the community or concerned parents. Staff is to refer to the principal or principal's designee for any media requests.
o Provide teachers with permission to allow students to express their feelings in class should the need arise. Review the need to stick to the facts, to refrain from speculating, and to preserve the deceased student's dignity and his/her parents' privacy.
o Compile list of students close to the deceased.
o Compile list of staff members who had contact with the deceased.
o Compile list of students who may be at risk of suicide.
o Remind staff about risk factors and warning signs of youth suicide.
o Provide staff with counseling opportunities and support services. Recommended
source: www.sprc.org/resources-programs/after-suicide-toolkit-schools

Tool 22: Additional Postvention Steps After a Suicide

Additional Postvention Steps
1. Verify the death has occurred and determine the cause of death
2. Mobilize the School Crisis Response Team
3. Assess the suicide's impact on the school and estimate the level of postvention response needed
4. Notify school staff in person if possible and provide support

5. Contact the family of the suicide victim
☐ Contact should be made in person and as soon as possible but certainly within 24 hours of the death
☐ Purposes include:
    ○ Express sympathy
    ○ Offer support
    ○ Identify the victim's siblings and friends who need assistance,
    ○ Discuss the school's postvention response
    ○ Identify details about the death that can be shared with outsiders,
    ○ Discuss funeral arrangements and whether the family wants school personnel and/or students to attend

6. Determine what information to share about the suicide
☐ Sample letters are available (www.afsp.org and www.sprc.org) to use as templates depending on the messaging:
    ○ Death has been ruled a suicide
    ○ Cause is unconfirmed (ask that rumors not be spread)
    ○ In the event the family has requested the cause of death not be disclosed, consider using the following phrasing in your letter to the school or community: "There are rumors of suicide, and, since that subject has been raised, suicide is a leading cause of death for youth, and we must all know the warning signs of suicide and where to get help for ourselves or our friends. Suicide is very complex, but mental illnesses such as depression are usually the cause." If the family cannot be persuaded that it is the best interest of their child's friends and future prevention efforts to tell the truth about the suicide, that no family issues or factors would ever be shared, and that the focus will be to only support the living, then it is recommended that the school crisis team convene. At that time, the school crisis team will decide whether to follow the recommendations about disclosure of the cause of death. These recommendations are found in *After a Suicide: A Toolkit for Schools*.

7. Determine how to share information about the death
☐ It is recommended students be told the truth about the cause of death in classrooms or smaller groups (not over the PA system) and the focus be on how to help the survivors with their emotions.
    ○ The answer as to why the suicide occurred died with the victim
    ○ No one person and no one thing was the cause of the suicide
    ○ Suicide is very complex, and the deceased traveled a long road, and mental illness is almost always involved when a suicide occurs

- It is strongly recommended that discussion with students after a suicide be in a group no larger than a classroom with a school counselor leading the discussion and the classroom teacher closely monitoring student reactions
- No school-wide assemblies should be held after a suicide as it will glamorize the death, students will be unlikely to ask questions, and student reactions to the suicide will be difficult to monitor

8. Identify students significantly affected by the suicide and provide support and initiate referral for community services as needed
   - Risk factors for imitative behavior:
     - Facilitated the suicide by encouragement or provided the lethal means
     - Failed to recognize the suicidal intent
     - Believe they may have caused the suicide
     - Had a relationship with the suicide victim
     - Identify with the suicide victim
     - Have a history of prior suicidal behavior
     - Have a history of psychopathology
     - Show symptoms of helplessness and/or hopelessness
     - Have suffered significant life stressors or losses
     - Lack internal and external protective resources

9. Conduct a staff planning session as soon as possible, and if school is not in session, utilize the staff calling tree to provide staff the opportunity to work through their own issues and turn to significant others for help

10. Initiate crisis-intervention services

11. Memorials
    - Strive to treat all student deaths the same way and create memorialization procedures so that all deaths are treated the same regardless of cause of death or factors such as socio-economics or popularity
      - Encourage and allow students, with parental permission, to attend the funeral
      - Encourage staff attendance at the funeral to support the family and monitor reactions of students
      - Contribute to a suicide-prevention effort in the community
      - Develop living memorials, such as student assistance programs, that address risk factors in local youth
    - Prohibiting all memorials is problematic
      - Recognize the challenge to strike a balance between the needs of distraught students and fulfilling the primary purpose of education
      - Meet with students and be creative and compassionate
      - Spontaneous memorials at school should be left in place until after the funeral
    - Avoid holding funeral services on school grounds and suggest the funeral be held after school so parents can accompany their children
    - Schools may hold supervised gatherings such as candlelight memorials
    - Monitor student gatherings off campus
    - Student newspaper coverage should follow media reporting guidelines available at www.afsp.org
    - Yearbook and graduation dedication or tributes should all be treated the same regardless of the cause of death for the student

- Grieving friends and family should be discouraged from dedicating a school event and guided instead towards promoting suicide prevention
- Permanent memorials on campus are discouraged, but schools need to memorialize all students the same way regardless of the cause of death, so if a precedent has already been set for planting a tree on campus, then it should be continued.

12. Social media
    - Name a Social Media Manager to assist the Public Information Officer
    - Utilize students as "cultural brokers" to help faculty and staff understand the social media that is currently most used by students
    - Train students in gatekeeper role and specifically identify what suicide risk looks like when communicated via social media
    - Have staff monitor social networks and provide safe messaging when important (this will require that districts not completely block these networks). Safe messaging (see Tools 25 and 26) stresses that suicide is preventable and largely the result of mental illness, and that evidence-based treatments exist for mental illness.
    - Encourage parents to monitor their child's social media
    - Psychoeducation: Make use of social media to post prevention messages, crisis support lines, and community mental health resources
    - Direct parents and students to the suicide-prevention information posted on the district website (see Tool 29)
    - Give students specific helpful language to include when making use of social media
    - Work with YouTube and Facebook to take down messages with disturbing images or language
    - Utilize the Facebook application to report concerns or issues with content

13. Debrief the postvention response with school crisis team members and identify needed additional actions

14. The suicide of a student during a school break or near the end of the school year creates challenges for schools to provide needed support for siblings and classmates. It is recommended that key personnel such as school counselors do their best to monitor and support students over school breaks with phone contact and follow up as they strive for continuing mental health care in the community

15. There is often an anniversary effect to suicide as students have attempted or died by suicide on the birthday that the suicide victim would have had, on the anniversary of their death, or at graduation time. School personnel are encouraged to be alert to these milestone dates and to reach out to students that have been identified as having the most difficulty in the aftermath of the suicide.

16. Schools need to be familiar with suicide survivor groups and locate the nearest one in their region of Montana as participation in group sessions with others who lost their loved ones to suicide is very beneficial

Tool 23: Sample Agenda for Initial All-Staff Meeting

This meeting is typically conducted by the Crisis Response Team Leader and should be held as soon as possible, ideally before school starts in the morning.

Depending on when the death occurs, there may not be enough time to hold the meeting before students have begun to hear the news through word of mouth, text messaging, or other means. If this happens, the Crisis Response Team Leader should first verify the accuracy of the reports and then notify staff of the death through the school's predetermined crisis alert system, such as e-mail or calls to classroom phones.

Remember that information about the cause of death should be withheld until the family has been consulted.

Goals of Initial Meeting

Allow at least one hour to address the following goals:

- ☐ Introduce the Crisis Response Team members
- ☐ Share accurate information about the death
- ☐ Allow staff an opportunity to express their own reactions and grief. Identify anyone who may need additional support and refer them to appropriate resources.
- ☐ Provide appropriate faculty (e.g., homeroom teachers or advisors) with a scripted death notification statement for students. Arrange coverage for any staff who are unable to manage reading the statement.
- ☐ Prepare for student reactions and questions by providing handouts to staff on Talking About Suicide (Tool 24) and Facts About Suicide and Mental Disorders in Adolescents (Tool 11).
- ☐ Explain plans for the day, including locations of crisis-counseling rooms
- ☐ Remind all staff of the important role they may play in identifying changes in behavior among the students they know and see every day, and discuss plans for handling students who are having difficulty
- ☐ Brief staff about identifying and referring at-risk students as well as about the need to keep records of those efforts
- ☐ Apprise staff of any outside crisis responders or others who will be assisting
- ☐ Remind staff of student dismissal protocol for funeral
- ☐ Identify which Crisis Response Team member has been designated as the media spokesperson and instruct staff to refer all media inquiries to him or her

Meeting at the End of the First Day

It can be helpful for the Crisis Response Team Leader and/or the Team Coordinator to have an all-staff meeting at the end of the first day. This meeting provides an opportunity to take the following steps:

- ☐ Offer verbal appreciation of the staff
- ☐ Review the day's challenges and successes
- ☐ Debrief, share experiences, express concerns, and ask questions
- ☐ Check in with staff to assess whether any of them need additional support and refer accordingly

- ☐ Disseminate information regarding the death and/or funeral arrangements
- ☐ Discuss plans for the next day
- ☐ Remind staff of the importance of self-care
- ☐ **Remind staff of the importance of documenting crisis-response efforts for future planning and understanding**

Source: *After a Suicide Toolkit.* AFSP and SPRC, www.sprc.org/resources-programs/after-suicide-toolkit-schools.

Tool 24: Talking About Suicide

Give Accurate Information About Suicide

Suicide is a complicated behavior. It is *not* caused by a single event such as a bad grade, an argument with parents, or the breakup of a relationship.

In most cases, suicide is caused by an underlying mental disorder like depression or substance abuse. Mental disorders affect the way people feel and prevent them from thinking clearly and rationally. Having a mental disorder is nothing to be ashamed of, and help is available.

Talking about suicide in a calm, straightforward manner does not put ideas into kids' minds.

Address blaming and scapegoating.

It is common to try to answer the question "why?" after a suicide death. Sometimes, this turns into blaming others for the death.

Do not focus on the method or on graphic details.

Talking in graphic detail about the method can create images that are upsetting and can increase the risk of imitative behavior by vulnerable youth.

If asked, it is okay to give basic facts about the method, but do not give graphic details or talk at length about it. The focus should be not on how someone killed themselves but on how to cope with feelings of sadness, loss, anger, etc.

Examples of Talking Points

"The cause of _____'s death was suicide. Suicide is most often caused by serious mental disorders like depression, combined with other complications."

"_____was likely struggling with a mental health issue like depression or anxiety, even though it may not have been obvious to other people."

"There are treatments to help people who are having suicidal thoughts."

"Since 90 percent of people who die by suicide have a mental disorder at the time of their death, it is likely that _____ suffered from a mental disorder that affected [his/her] feelings, thoughts, and ability to think clearly and solve problems in a better way."

"Mental disorders are not something to be ashamed of, and there are very good treatments to help the symptoms go away."

"The reasons that someone dies by suicide are complicated and are related to mental disorders that get in the way of the person thinking clearly. Blaming others—or blaming the person who died—does not acknowledge the reality that the person was battling a mental disorder."

"It is tragic that he died by hanging. Let's talk about how _____'s death has affected you and ways for you to handle it."

"How can we figure out the best ways to deal with our loss and grief?"

Source: *After a Suicide: A Toolkit for Schools,* www.sprc.org/resources-programs/after-suicide-toolkit-schools

Tool 25: Key Messages for Media Spokesperson

For use when fielding media inquiries

Suicide/Mental Illness

Depression is the leading cause of suicide in teenagers.

About 6 percent of teenagers will develop depression yearly. Sadly, more than 80 percent of these kids will not have their illness properly diagnosed or treated, which can also lead to school absenteeism, failing grades, dropouts, crimes, and drug and alcohol abuse.

Depression is among the most treatable of all mood disorders. More than three-fourths of people with depression respond positively to treatment.

The best way to prevent suicide is through early detection, diagnosis, and vigorous treatment of depression and other mental disorders, including addictions.

School's Response Messages

We are heartbroken over the death of one of our students. Our hearts, thoughts, and prayers go out to [his/her] family and friends and the entire community.

We will be offering grief counseling for students, faculty, and staff starting on [date] through [date].

We will be hosting an informational meeting for parents and the community regarding suicide prevention on [date/time/location]. Experts will be on hand to answer questions.

No TV cameras or reporters will be allowed in the school or on school grounds.

School Response to Media

Media are strongly encouraged to refer to the document "Reporting on Suicide: Recommendations for the Media," which is available at www.afsp.org/media and www.sprc.org/resources-programs/recommendations-reporting-suicide.

Research has shown that graphic, sensationalized, or romanticized descriptions of suicide deaths in the news media can contribute to suicide contagion ("copycat" suicides), particularly among youth.

Media coverage that details the location and manner of suicide with photos or video increases risk of contagion.

Media should also avoid oversimplifying cause of suicide (e.g., "student took his own life after breakup with girlfriend"). This gives the audience a simplistic understanding of a very complicated issue.

Instead, remind the public that more than 90 percent of people who die by suicide have an underlying mental disorder such as depression.

Media should include links to or information about helpful resources such as local crisis hotlines or the National Suicide Prevention Lifeline 800-273-TALK (8255).

Tool 26: Sample Media Statement

(To be provided to local media outlets either upon request or proactively.)

School personnel were informed by the coroner's office that a [___]-year-old student at [_____] school has died. The cause of death was suicide.

Our thoughts and support go out to [his/her] family and friends at this difficult time.

The school will be hosting a meeting for parents and others in the community at [date/time/location]. Members of the school's Crisis Response Team [or mental health professionals] will be present to provide information about common reactions following a suicide and how adults can help youths cope. They will also provide information about suicide and mental illness in adolescents, including risk factors and warning signs of suicide, and they will address attendees' questions and concerns. A meeting announcement has been sent to parents, who can contact school administrators or counselors at [number] or [e-mail address] for more information.

Trained crisis counselors will be available to meet with students and staff starting tomorrow and continuing over the next few weeks as needed.

Suicide Warning Signs

These signs may mean someone is at risk for suicide. Risk is greater if a behavior is new or has recently increased in frequency or intensity, and if it seems related to a painful event, loss, or change.

- Talking about wanting to die or kill oneself
- Looking for ways to kill oneself, such as searching online or buying a gun
- Talking about feeling hopeless or having no reason to live
- Talking about feeling trapped or in unbearable pain
- Talking about being a burden to others
- Increasing the use of alcohol or drugs
- Acting anxious or agitated or behaving recklessly
- Sleeping too little or too much
- Withdrawing or feeling isolated
- Showing rage or talking about seeking revenge
- Displaying extreme mood swings

Local Community Mental Health Resources

[To be inserted by school]

National Suicide Prevention Lifeline

800-273-TALK (8255)

[Local hotline numbers to be inserted by school]

(Source: AFSP & SPRC: *After a Suicide: A Toolkit for Schools*)

Tool 27: Caring for the Caregiver—Promoting Healing

Self-care is always important—even more so when going through difficult and tragic times. There are many things students (and adults.) can do to care for themselves. Remember that, as everyone grieves differently, strategies for healing are unique for each individual. Some of these will work for you, and some will not. When we are feeling stressed and overwhelmed, it can be difficult to think of what to do, so here are some suggestions to ease the burden of having to think about what to do next.

Be Healthy

Drink plenty of water and eat well

Limit alcohol and caffeine

Exercise to release endorphins and decrease stress: try yoga or go for a walk, hike, or bike ride

Mental Escapes/Take a Break

Do things you enjoy. If you can't think of anything right now, ask someone what you used to enjoy. Do it even if it sounds like too much right now.

What are your guilty pleasures? Do them.

Enjoy all that nature has to offer

Rest and Relaxation: light a candle, take a bubble bath, and get a massage

Swim: water can be therapeutic

Play with your favorite pet

Hold a baby (then give him/her back to the parent if he/she isn't yours). Play with a child.

Meditate

Watch a funny TV show (but not too much and not right before bed)

Laughter is the best medicine: hang out with your funniest friend

Watch a pleasurable/funny movie

Read a page-turner

Internal Coping

Write lists of gratitude

Be easy on yourself

Give yourself permission to feel/grieve

Accept yourself

Remember that this is hard and takes time

Don't blame yourself

External Coping

Reach out to others to talk: professionals, colleagues, friends, family, clergy (make sure these are people you trust)

Attend a religious service

Ask for a hug

Expressive Activities

Communication is 90% nonverbal: dance, sing, cry, perform, and draw

Listen to (or create) relaxing/soothing music

Write in a journal

Write poetry

Maintain Structure	
Eat, sleep, and pray at regular times Plan your day	Keep as normal a routine as possible (though this may be a *new* normal)

Tool 28: Screening Mental Health Providers

The following questions can be asked of mental health service providers to help you get an idea of whether they would be able to meet the needs of students at risk of suicide.

These questions were drawn on the authors' professional experiences and adapted from the SAMHSA Toolkit (2012).

Professional Qualifications

1. Are you able to provide services to children and adolescents?
2. Are there ages that you work more frequently with or have more expertise and training with?
3. What types of services do you provide?
4. Do you do individual, family, couples, or group therapy?
5. Do you have experience working with LGBTQ students and other groups that are disproportionately at risk for suicide?
6. Do you have experience working with varied cultural, ethnic, and religious groups found within our community?
7. Do you have experience assessing suicide risk in youth? If yes, where did you get your training?
8. Do you have experience managing and treating suicide risk in youth? If yes, what treatment approach do you use? Do you have training in any empirically supported treatments for suicidal youth (e.g., cognitive behavioral therapy, dialectical behavior therapy, interpersonal psychotherapy, attachment-based family therapy)?
9. Do you have experience working with people who have lost a loved one to suicide?
10. What process do you follow in the event of a suicide crisis?
11. Under what circumstances would you come to the school or do a home visit in order to see a student or parent?
12. Do you work with a psychiatrist?

Business Issues

1. Where are you located?
2. Are you accessible via public transportation?
3. What is your typical wait time to see a new client?
4. What insurance do you accept?
5. Do you have a sliding fee scale for people who pay out of pocket? What is the range of the fee scale?
6. Do you have necessary clearances to work in schools if you were to come here—child abuse, police, and FBI clearances?

Source: Substance Abuse and Mental Health Services Administration (2012): *Preventing Suicide: A Toolkit for High Schools.* HHS Publication No.SMA-12-4669. Rockville, MD: Center for Mental Health Services, Substance Abuse and Mental Health Services Administration.
Retrieved from store.samhsa.gov/product/Preventing-Suicide-A-Toolkit-for-High-Schools/SMA12-4669 (Toolkit 2.A, p.68)

Tool 29: Suicide-Prevention Information for Posting on School District Website

The_____School District recognizes that suicide is the second leading cause of death for school- age students in Montana, and we are dedicated to working with parents, community agencies, and state agencies to prevent youth suicide. The suicide of a youth is largely the result of untreated or undertreated metal illness, and we as a district have developed plans for suicide prevention and intervention.

If you are a student and concerned about your friend, it is very important to get a trusted adult involved immediately. If you are a parent concerned about your child, obtain professional help for your child, increase your supervision, and remove any lethal means from their ready access. Many people are hesitant to ask directly about suicide for fear that they will be planting the idea in the mind of the person. Asking them directly about thoughts of suicide provides them an opportunity to unburden themselves and to receive the support and services they need.

The key person to contact in our district for assistance is_____, who can be reached at _____. If they cannot be reached immediately, call the National Suicide Prevention Lifeline at 1-800-SUICIDE (784-2433) or 1-800-273-TALK (8255) or text "MT" to 741741 (a free 24/7 text line for people in crisis) where trained crisis responders are available 24 hours a day. Do not leave a suicidal individual alone. If a suicide attempt has been made, immediately contact 911.

Additional suicide-prevention information is available at the Montana Department of Public Health and Human Services (DPHHS) website: dphhs.mt.gov/amdd/suicide.

It is vital that all school staff, parents, and community members know that suicide can be prevented and know the warning signs of suicide:

- Talking about suicide
- Making statements about feeling hopeless, helpless, or worthless
- A deepening depression
- History of mental illness
- Preoccupation with death
- Taking unnecessary risks or exhibiting self-destructive behavior
- Engaging in non-suicidal self-injury
- Being victimized by bullying
- Out-of-character behavior, dramatic changes in behavior
- A loss of interest in the things one cares about
- Visiting or calling people one cares about in a way that hints at saying goodbye
- Making arrangements, setting one's affairs in order
- Giving prized possessions away
- Exposure to suicide

The American Association of Suicidology (www.suicidology.org) provides the following warning signs in an acronym form:

IS PATH WARM?

I Ideation

S Substance Abuse

P Purposelessness

A Anxiety

T Trapped

H Hopelessness

W Withdrawal

A Anger

R Recklessness

M Mood Changes

Tool 30: Update on Montana CAST-S Implementation

School:	
Has the school/district identified a suicide-prevention specialist? Please provide the email address of whom we could contact when new information and/or resources become available.	☐ Yes ☐ No
What suicide-prevention training have you implemented for all district staff?	
What training has been provided on suicide assessment for personnel (i.e., counselors)?	
What protocols have you established for parent notification and referral for suicidal students?	
Have you identified mental health resources in your community or region?	☐ Yes ☐ No
How have you linked with community resources for suicide prevention?	
What information have you shared with parents about their role in suicide prevention?	
Share your suicide-prevention accomplishments at your school or in your school district.	
Have you had a student die by suicide?	☐ Yes ☐ No
Do you have a suicide postvention plan?	☐ Yes ☐ No
What additional support do you need in your district to improve prevention efforts?	
Send this Implementation Update form to: DPHHS, SAM, NAMI, and Big Sky AACAP	

Tool 31: Identification of Mental Health Facilities and Providers

Mental Health Providers in Your Community and/or Region for a Suicidal Crisis		
Identify facilities and providers available locally or regionally. List contact phone and address.		
Provider:	Phone:	Address:
Has a staff member at the facility or the office been identified as a contact for emergency situations? If so, who?	☐ Yes ☐ No _____	
Does the facility provide transport for suicidal individuals?	☐ Yes ☐ No	
Has the school system used the facility or the provider previously?	☐ Yes ☐ No	
Was the facility or the provider responsive when contacted?	☐ Yes ☐ No	
Were the student and his or her family satisfied with the services?	☐ Yes ☐ No	
Did the facility or the provider communicate effectively with the school/district and attempt to coordinate care for the suicidal student?	☐ Yes ☐ No	

Tool 32: Memorandum of Understanding (Outline)

Information Sharing for Schools, Agencies, and Outside Mental Health Professionals

Suggested outline of components of the document

Purpose

This Memorandum of Understanding (MOU) is entered into by and between …

Objective/agreement

Form: Authorization and Consent to Disclosure and Exchange of Information

Utilization of the authorization form

Identification of personnel who will oversee the process and serve as coordinator of referrals and resources

State conditions for securing confidential information and sharing with authorized individuals

Legal compliance/re-disclosure

The parties agree and acknowledge that each and all of them remain individually responsible for complying with the laws, rules, and/or regulations that pertain to their specific operations, etc.

Term/participation/initial participation

Identification of confidentiality laws, rules, and regulations

Authorization and consent to disclosure and exchange of information form

Participation acknowledgement

The following agency/mental health professional or entity hereby acknowledges its participation in and agreement with the terms.

Agency/professional: _____

_____

Authorizing official: _____

_____

Telephone number: _____

E-mail: _____

APPENDICES

Appendix 1: Parent Questions and Answers

Answers to Parent Questions about Parenting, Suicide Prevention

and Promoting Student Mental Health and Resilience

from Dr. Scott Poland

1. **How much does academic pressure affect kids (parent or school)?**
There are a multitude of problems that contribute to the factors of youth suicide, and epidemiology studies done by the Center for Disease Control have identified a number of factors. Those factors include family problems, substance abuse, academic pressure, access to lethal means, and issues that have to do with harassment and bullying (especially for LGBTQ students). In looking at all these factors together, the most significant one is mental illness and most likely depression.

2. **What support can we offer to students who are not part of the majority population (an atheist in a largely Christian community, for example)?**
It is very important that all of our schools and communities be very embracing of all students regardless of their ethnicity, race, religious views, and sexual orientation. The hallmark characteristic of a Christian community should be acceptance and support of all community members regardless of their religious affiliation or the level of their beliefs. I believe it is very important that the community be very embracing and reach out to all students and let them know that they are accepted.

3. **Why do you think the suicide rate is so high in Montana?**
The suicide rate in Montana, in general, is high. In the latest figures from the American Association of Suicidology, Montana was listed as number three in America with regards to suicide rates. The states with the highest risk for suicide are all in the west—states like Alaska, Wyoming, Washington, Idaho, and Colorado. There have been many theories about why these western states have high suicide rates. A number of these states have a large percentage of American Indians, with high suicide rates. With regards to the state of Montana, it has been referenced that the rural nature, the lack of mental health resources, the stigma that is still associated with getting help for yourself or a member of your family that has a mental illness, as well as gun access have all been identified as critical issues. There is another theory that has been advanced called the "elevation theory." Although there is not definitive research on this,
there is some evidence that antidepressants may not be as effective when they are taken at high elevations, and that oxygen deprivation affects brain chemistry. I think it is really important to emphasize that other locations in the nation have also been singled out for having high youth-suicide rates. I personally have worked in the aftermath of high suicide rates and contagion in the last few years in New Smyrna Beach, FL, Fairfax County, VA; Colorado Springs, CO; St.

Joseph, MO; and Palo Alto, CA. It's very important that we recognize that Montana is not alone in facing this problem, and that the local community, state, and school leaders are collaborating and taking many concrete steps to prevent further youth suicides.

4. **Do you know of any specific filtering software/apps that you have found to be effective with teens?**

There are a number of applications for both smartphones and computers that can help parents be more aware of websites that their teens are visiting and communications they are receiving. I think the most important piece of advice I can give in answering this question is that The Classical Academy has technology specialists who can respond and provide more specific information to answer this question. The one point I'd like to make is that not all parents are going to need these applications. They especially need to be used when a parent is excessively concerned about their child's behavior and him/her being consumed by technology. In addition, there may be parents who are concerned about the negative influence other children are having on their own child. In all of these cases, when concerns reach a critical level, I would strongly recommend counseling for your child in addition to using these applications. The counseling department in Montana schools can certainly make referrals to the best providers in the area.

5. **How do I find a good mental health practitioner specifically for tweens and teens?**

There are many mental health practitioners who specialize in working with children and adolescents. My recommendation is to contact the counseling department at your child's school because school counselors are very familiar with practitioners who specialize in working with upper elementary students and adolescents.

6. **Are children who have a stay-at-home parent at a lower risk for suicide?**

Children who have a stay-at-home parent are very fortunate in many respects as there will be more opportunities for parent and child interactions and increased supervision. The research from the World Health Organization has not specifically emphasized having a stay-at-home parent as a protective factor but instead stressed the following factors that prevent youth suicide: stable families, access to mental health treatment, lack of access to lethal weapons, positive self-esteem, good relations with other youth, and religious involvement.

7. **What social media sites should my junior-high student be allowed to join?**

Social media is a major issue for junior high school students. It is important that parents are very familiar with the media sites that their children are visiting. Technology is a privilege, not a right. It is the parents who are paying for the monthly telephone bills and the Wi-Fi that is available in your home. You do have a right to know what sites your child visits. After visiting the sites and becoming familiar with them, you are in a better position to determine if the site is a healthy one and one that you are comfortable with your child viewing. When you have questions about the developmental appropriateness of the site, and you cannot determine this on your own, I suggest that you contact the counseling department at your child's school and ask them their opinion.

8. **Which social media sites are dangerous for teens?**

In the answer to question 7, I made the point that parents need to visit the websites their children are accessing and make their own determination whether these sites are healthy or not. I believe the other important factor is to examine the overall well-being of your child. For example, I am often asked, "My child likes to visit this particular website as they are fascinated with media violence. Should I be concerned?" I'm going to ask a number of questions, and if I find out that the student in question is involved in at least one organized activity, they go somewhere with Mom and Dad once in a while, they do a good job taking care of the family pet, they apologize when they hurt someone's feelings, and they show empathy for other people, then I am going to relax. Those are very healthy behaviors for a young person. However, if the young person visits violent and very unhealthy websites, they do not apologize or show remorse, they are fascinated with violence/guns/bombs, they in fact tried to harm the family pet, and they are totally isolated from all adults, now I am very concerned. Those behaviors collectively and additively are extremely troubling signs for young people. The important point is to not be overly concerned with a fascination with one subject or the frequent visiting of a social network site that the parents don't necessarily approve of. The most important thing is the overall adjustment of your child. If you are concerned and there are many red flags, please consider obtaining counseling for your child and increasing your supervision. And, yes, I would encourage "snooping" with regards to room, websites visited, journals, diaries, etc., when you observe a number of these concerning behaviors.

9. **What causes cluster suicides?**

Clusters of suicides fall into two categories. Mass clusters have been researched extensively since the 1700s. A mass cluster might occur when a celebrity or a known national figure dies by suicide. There is not a lot of research support for mass suicide clusters. For example, the suicide of Robin Williams approximately two years ago, a very beloved American actor, thankfully did not result in an increased suicide rate in America. His suicide did result in an increased number of calls to suicide hotlines for assistance, which was a very good outcome. Point clusters refer to more suicides than we would expect in a short space of time in one geographical region. It is well-known that teenagers are more susceptible to imitating suicidal behavior than any other age group. Exposure to suicide has been added as a suicide risk factor. I think of it this way: the suicide of a young person is like throwing a rock into a pond, causing a ripple effect in the schools, communities, and churches. This ripple effect is greater than ever before today because of social networks. Vulnerable youths find each other online. Schools have had a tendency to think that the suicide only affected their one school when, in reality, throughout the area, students in many middle schools and high schools are affected. I would like to, in particular, compliment the state of Montana for all of their efforts for suicide prevention. There's been collaboration between schools, agencies, mental health providers, law enforcement, the medical community, and survivor groups. There has been information provided for both school staff, students, and parents. Essentially, youth suicide prevention must involve the entire village, as no single entity or agency can do enough about it alone. It is essential that suicide information be shared with everybody concerned, and that everyone understands suicide is not fate, nor is it destiny, and the vast majority of youth suicides can and should be prevented.

10. **Are teens capable of hiding depression?**

There are a number of clear warning signs of teenage depression. Parents have reported that they are often confused as to whether it is really depression or typical teenage moodiness, irritability, and angst. Here are the key things that parents need to be looking for: First, is this pervasive? That means, is it affecting all aspects of your child's life? School and academic performance? Peer and social relationships? Family relationships? Is this behavior persistent? That means, has it gone on for two or three weeks or more? The next thing the parent needs to consider is whether their child has dropped out of activities that were previously pleasurable to them. For example, your son enjoyed playing basketball for years, but this year he's decided not to go out for the team. Or, your daughter has enjoyed playing volleyball or has been on the dance team for years, and now, suddenly, she has lost interest in those activities. I believe it is vitally important that parents be involved in all aspects of their child's life, and, if you pay attention to these factors, I do not think that an adolescent is going to be able to hide their state of depression from you. If they are isolating themselves in their room, they are having problems with their sleep cycle, they don't want to have meals with the family, or they are not involved in social activities at previous levels, then I believe you know, as a parent, something is wrong. Please, do not hesitate to seek professional help for your child. It is estimated that 20% of all teenagers suffer from depression at some point during those tumultuous years. It is also concerning that a review of the literature says that 80% of depressed teenagers never receive any treatment whatsoever. The treatment needed, very likely, will involve cognitive behavior or talk therapy and antidepressant medications. Many professionals, including myself, believe that the "black box warning" on antidepressants for adolescents has resulted in many adolescents who desperately needed those medications not receiving them. We also believe that not receiving needed medication has contributed to the increase in suicide rates for adolescents as

it is now their second leading cause of death. This may be affected by parental reluctance for their child to receive antidepressant medication and a lack of information about their effectiveness. I believe strongly that a careful diagnosis of depression needs to be made, and medication needs to be monitored frequently. I specifically request that medications be monitored weekly for the first month after an adolescent starts taking an antidepressant. If your child is on an antidepressant, and you or your child are not pleased with the medication, please go back and talk to the prescribing physician and share your concerns.

11. **How can we engage parents who are in denial or who don't want to talk about suicide in our community?**

Suicide is a very difficult topic. In my career, I have found many parents, school leaders, and even personal friends and colleagues very reluctant to talk about suicide. Many people believe the myth that if we talk about suicide, we will plant the idea in their mind, and they will think about it for the first time ever. Nothing could be further from the truth. Our U.S. Surgeon General commented, "More than 44,000 suicides happen annually in this country. We need to talk about this more in our homes, our schools, our churches, and our communities."

Unfortunately, many students in Montana personally know someone who died by suicide. Although our initial thoughts are that we shouldn't bring it up, in reality, because these suicides have occurred, we need to talk about it more. This discussion should always focus on prevention and utilizing national and state crisis hotlines such as 1-800-SUICIDE, 1-800-273-TALK, or 877-542-7233. Young people today are very in tune with texting, and therefore it is important that they are all aware of the national Crisis Text Line (www.crisistextline.org). To utilize the crisis text line, simply text "MT" to 741741. If you are aware of a family in your community that is very hesitant to talk about suicide, then the best way to open that conversation is through listening. Try a simple question like, "I'm really sorry that suicides have affected your family. How can I help?" The more you can be in a listening mode and, hopefully, be able to mention the key points that I brought up in the beginning of this question the better, as it is really important that we address the most common myth that we plant the idea of suicide in someone's head if we talk about suicide. The greatest problem we have that limits suicide prevention is the misinformation and the myths surrounding this subject.

12. **Is there any significance to the location that a student chooses for a suicide attempt?**

The vast majority of youth suicides occur in their own home, after school hours, and when their family members are most likely to be in the home. I've always believed that most suicidal individuals do, in fact, want to be stopped, and they set it up hoping that someone will figure out what they are thinking, that they are experiencing unendurable pain, are not thinking clearly, and see no alternatives or a way out. Very rarely does a suicide occur at school; however, this has happened in a number of schools in our country. My response to a suicide happening at school would be to not make a dramatic conclusion about the location that was chosen but instead to focus on the young person, who very likely wanted to be stopped and hoped that someone would be able to figure out the extent of their pain.

13. **Are tattoos and/or piercings a safe and culturally acceptable way of cutting?**

Tattoos and piercings, especially for the younger generation, have become socially approved and sanctioned. I am old-fashioned and believe that children need to discuss with their parents whether getting a tattoo or piercing is acceptable within the family. I emphasized earlier the importance of parents being involved in their child's life. What I really hope is that there is free and easy communication around the dinner table several nights a week. I emphasize in my parenting presentations that we need to bring the family meal back. It's not a visit to a fast food restaurant—it's around your kitchen table. Therefore, if you are tuned in, a good listener, and really involved in your child's life, hopefully they will share with you any thoughts they are having about getting a tattoo or piercing. I think it's very important that I distinguish tattoos and piercings from injurious behaviors, also referred to as non-suicidal self-injury. NSSI is a coping mechanism. It is one that young people engage in when they are experiencing anxiety and they are overwhelmed with things that are going on in their life. The most common forms of NSSI are cutting or burning, which results in a moderate or superficial injury to their skin. This behavior has biological and psychological benefits. The psychological benefits are of regulation. They can shut out the humiliation they just experienced, a major disappointment, or perhaps the argument their parents are having in the other room. The biological benefits are that endorphins are released that are the very same ones that are released through exercise. So, there are clearly biological and psychological benefits to engaging in NSSI. If a young person gets a tattoo or a piercing, this is something they have thought about and planned over days, weeks, or even months. Self-injurious behavior (i.e., cutting and burning) is usually done impulsively following a precipitating event, such as arguments, humiliating events, etc. Therefore, these behaviors are very different. On one hand, to obtain a piercing or a tattoo you are making an appointment, traveling to a location, deciding on the piercing location, or deciding on the exact tattoo. On the other hand, self-injury with cutting and burning can be done immediately in isolation from other people. So, all one has to do is go into the bedroom or school bathroom, isolate oneself from others, and quickly engage in the behavior. It is important that we

recognize that a young person engaging in NSSI is getting comfortable with harming their body, and estimates are that 30% of those who engage repetitively in NSSI ultimately make a suicide attempt.

14. What input should teens have when it comes to the programs that schools select for suicide prevention?

This question really refers to suicide-prevention initiatives and the importance of getting input from teenagers themselves. First, I highly recommend that schools as much as possible utilize programs that are listed on the SAMHSA website as National Registry of Evidence-based Programs and Practices (NREPP) separates all existing programs into "Legacy programs" (nrepp.samhsa.gov/AdvancedSearch.aspx#aLegacyPrograms).

However, I also recommend that teenagers who have been affected by suicide be provided opportunities to promote suicide prevention. This could be through promoting crisis hotline resources. In addition, it is possible for older teenagers to go through training for participation in teen crisis lines in larger cities. In addition to raising money and awareness, teenagers can memorialize their friend with a "living memorial." The living memorial doesn't involve permanent shrines or markers or planting trees. It concentrates on promoting awareness, designating key mental health resources in our community, emphasizing depression as being treatable, and the fact that many teenagers suffer from depression in those tumultuous years. To summarize, administrators in Montana schools can contact OPI, SAM, and DPHHS for guidance as to which suicide-prevention programs they should initiate at their school. However, teenagers do need to be involved and have input in the memorialization and suicide-prevention resources, and, most importantly, they must be able to debunk the many myths associated with suicide. Suicide is not fate or destiny, and the actions of any one person may make all the difference in the world in preventing a suicide. Student initiatives are important, and I am aware there have been a number of those. One example was based on the motto "Keep on

Swimming." Students decorated and colored fish and posted them on the walls of their school. The message is really important: No matter what happens, we need to get help for ourselves and our friends, go on with our lives, and face whatever adversity comes along, knowing we're going to get the help we need.

15. Should schools promote social and emotional wellness?

Absolutely. I practiced as a psychologist full-time in schools for 25 years and have been concerned that too much focus in recent years has been on student academic performance and overall school academic ratings. I strongly support the theory of Abraham Maslow, who in his hierarchy of needs emphasized that the foundation for all of us is having our physical needs taken care of and feeling safe, secure, and a sense of belonging. National research has found that a very significant factor for overall adolescent well-being is whether they feel connected to their school. I hope that every student in Montana sincerely feels like someone at school cares if they show up today or not. I wrote an article for the American School Board Journal a number of years ago called "The Fourth R—Relationships." I now teach in a university, and I immediately learn my students' names, sincerely learn about their hopes and dreams, and focus on how I can help them be successful. I utilize many activities in my classes that I learned in my previous school position where, in addition to directing psychological services, I supervised the adventure-based outdoor counseling program that utilized high elements to build self-esteem and low elements to increase problem-solving and connections to others.

16. **How can I differentiate between "normal" stress/anxiety and teen depression?**

Please review my answer to question 10. In addition, this question brings up the term "anxiety." I think it is important that it be addressed from several avenues, including sleep deprivation. The research is very clear that, unfortunately, many adolescents are not getting enough sleep. A number of factors contribute to this, including the fact that teenagers are not wired to go to bed early, and the fact that many secondary schools in this country start too early. The national recommendation is that no secondary school start before 8:30 in the morning. One of the factors that contribute to teenagers' sleep deprivation is all of their technological devices. I suggest that parents decide the bedtime for their child and simply say, "I need your laptop now, I need your cell phone and iPad, and I will charge them and hand them back to you in the morning." National research has estimated that as many as one-third of teenagers wake up in the middle of the night to check what might have been posted about them. Taking charge of technology is something parents must do to ensure that their child is getting adequate sleep. Inadequate sleep is connected to anxiety, frustration, hopelessness, and depression for young people. Anxiety may also be the result of academic demands and pressure on young people. It was only a few years ago that a young person would be accepted to any state university of their choosing when they graduated from high school. Unfortunately, our flagship state universities have increased standards, so it might be necessary to be in the top 8% to 10% to be accepted into these universities. This has added a lot of pressure to young people as parents and grandparents were able to go to that flagship university where their own acceptance is in doubt, or they may have been turned down. I like to share with young people who are experiencing these difficulties that I did not make the top 25% of my own high school class in Kansas. And, in fact, later I was kicked out of the University of Kansas for poor scholarship. It took me a couple of years to find myself, and, frankly, military service helped. Today, I am proud to tell you that I have three degrees, including a doctoral degree, and have authored or coauthored five books. The sentiment that needs to be echoed by staff and parents is that not everything is going to work out perfectly. It is okay to go to a junior college. I actually attended two of them. After the student is more successful, they will be able to transfer to a college that may have been one of their top choices. The school district in Palo Alto, CA, has really wrestled with whether they should have "zero hour." When I was there, I asked, "What is zero hour?" and I was told it was an opportunity to go to school an hour before everyone else and take an extra AP class. My advice was to do away with zero hour, thereby lessening some of the academic pressure on students. At least, they initially eliminated it. However, zero hour is now back because parents with extremely high academic expectations for their children wanted them to be able to fit an extra AP class into their schedule. I believe that returning zero hour was a very unfortunate decision. I am obviously looking at the total well-being of our students and recommend, when possible, to lessen the academic pressure.

Some thoughts for the school and community are the following: Can we make certain that the various academic departments don't all give homework on the same night? For example, maybe Tuesday night is the English department, Thursday night is math, etc. A second suggestion would be to create a forum to allow students to log in to record the amount of time they are spending on each homework assignment. A parent and school committee could examine the number of hours spent on specific homework and make recommendations that could lessen some of the academic pressure. Please, also refer to my comments in question 10 regarding this issue, specifically with regards to anxiety. Perhaps your child is so anxious about a test in their class tomorrow, and you know they didn't eat well or sleep well, or they were up all night studying for the exam. Or perhaps they are telling you they can't go to school today because they are not ready for that important test. As a parent, you know your child the best, and if there is a consistent pattern of the behaviors I have just described, please don't hesitate to get professional help for your child and share concerns about academic expectations with your child's school administration.

17. **How do you walk the line between your child's privacy/freedom and keeping them safe?**
It is certainly a challenge to give your child privacy and balance your right to know and your concerns. It has been said that some adolescents are leading secret lives with regards to sex, drugs, and other dangerous behaviors. I have a couple of key thoughts on this.

One: I am a fan of desktop computer, meaning it's on the kitchen counter, it's in the family room, and your teenager needs access to that computer, but the websites they will be visiting, and the comments they will be posting, will be significantly different when you are going in and out of the room where that computer is located. Unfortunately, many parents "gave away the farm" when they gave their children access to technology in upper elementary school; it is hard to make changes later. If your child already has a laptop, the kitchen counter, family room, or dining room table needs to become their work space—not their bedroom where they probably have closed the door. In particular, I am extremely concerned about a laptop that contains a camera. Sexting has become a severe problem in this country. Most students are not aware that sending a picture of themselves nude to a classmate can still be prosecuted in some states—not as a misdemeanor but as a felony. I also know that sexting, being severely humiliated, and being taunted and teased by everyone at school for the picture that was sent out (not realizing it would be shared with everyone) was certainly a contributing factor to some suicides of young people. If you have a number of concerns about your child's behavior choices, then I believe you need to do a little snooping of online behavior, diaries, and journals. I would also highly recommend finding a shared time that your child will talk to you. I realize parents are extremely busy, but we have to make sure there are at least a few times each week when we are not distracted, we give our child individual attention, and we are in a listening mode. Then, hopefully, our children will share with us the frustration and challenges they are facing. If you remain concerned about their behavior with school, social life, and family, I suggest it is time to obtain private counseling. I am often asked, "Should it be up to my child whether or not they go to counseling?" My response is, "Absolutely not. Your 14-year-old is not in a good position to determine whether they need help." Simply say, "We are going to get counseling. Would you rather have a male or a female counselor?" Secondly, you could say, "I am happy to go with you and be in the meeting with you and your counselor, if you like. But, going is not up to you given my level of concern about the behaviors you are exhibiting." I'd like to also take a moment to emphasize I strongly believe that in Montana, where multiple youth suicides have occurred, all guns in homes need to be securely locked up. I'm aware of numerous situations where the parents believed that their child didn't know where they kept the gun, didn't know the combination to the safe, and didn't know where the bullets were stored. I am aware of tragedies that resulted from that. Please, take charge and secure your firearms: Your children have all been exposed to suicide, and that alone is a risk factor.

Two: The most dangerous thing your child engages in is riding in a car and driving a car. Make sure that you follow the graduated driving laws for Montana and be aware that the fatality rate for 16-year-olds is three times higher than for 18-year-olds in car accidents, and that is usually the result of inexperience—for example, not being familiar with driving after dark and being easily distracted when multiple friends are in the car. Take charge and model wearing your seat belts, never driving while intoxicated, and never talking or texting on your phone while you drive your car. If you do those things, why wouldn't your own children fail to wear a seatbelt, get in a car operated by someone clearly intoxicated, and talk and text while they are driving? The most frequent crisis that I have responded to throughout my career has been the many tragic car accidents that took the lives of our children. These car accidents can be prevented.

18. **How can a parent foster a culture of compassion/kindness with their elementary school child?**
Gandhi once said, "What we do speaks so loudly to our children that when we talk to them, they cannot hear us." This quote certainly stresses the importance of modeling. Modeling is especially important for compassion and kindness. As parents, ask yourselves, "How do I treat my partner in my home? How do I treat my neighbors? How do I respond when I interact with law enforcement when I've been stopped for speeding, having a tail light out, etc.? How do I respond in a teacher conference at school? How do I respond if I'm in the assistant principal's office because my child has exhibited a misbehavior?" These questions set the stage for our children. I believe strongly that when we model compassion by caring for everyone, regardless of their sexual orientation or their religious affiliation, we are setting the tone for our children to express kindness and compassion for everyone. I'm aware that Montana schools have a number of programs that emphasize kindness and compassion, and that they welcome parental input. A suggestion might be that parents ask that a task force be formed that would include school personnel who would look at kindness and compassion at school. When we address these subjects, we must also bring up the topic of bullying. Montana schools have policies and procedures and provide training to reduce bullying at all school levels. It is very important that

schools do the following: support the victim and make it clear that the victim does not deserve this, and the school will get it stopped and be there for them every step of the way. The bully needs to be told, "Here are the consequences for today…If this behavior continues, the consequences will escalate. It will not be kept a secret. All the other staff will be told about your bullying behavior, and they will be watching." It needs to be a teachable moment for the bystanders. Research has shown that the more bystanders are present, the less likely it is that someone will intervene. It has even been argued that the term "bystander" is too passive. The term needs to be replaced with "witness." When we are a witness to something, we feel responsible to report what took place. Reaching the bystanders/witnesses is the key to reducing bullying in our schools.

Empathy is important to address. Empathy involves envisioning and putting ourselves in someone else's shoes. When we can do that, we can envision what it would be like to be treated a certain way. Hopefully, parents discuss empathy with their children as opportunities might arise when watching a movie or television show or discussing something that happened at school. You could ask, "How do you think that person might have felt in that situation?" The parent can help the child envision and empathize with the thoughts that had to be going
through the movie character's or student's mind at the time.

19. **There is a high suicide rate for veterans in the United States. Are the children of these veterans at a higher risk?**

First and foremost, being a veteran myself, I'd like to thank everyone for their previous or current service. I'm very concerned about the number of suicides that have occurred for veterans and even for current active-duty personnel. *Time Magazine* had an article a number of years ago stating that 22 veterans die of suicide in America every single day. In addition, there have been articles describing the fact that more of our currently serving personnel die by suicide every year than die in combat. I'm aware of many military initiatives to prevent suicide and to destigmatize mental health treatment. But, I'm also aware that when high-ranking military professionals talk about being "army strong," they really mean that you don't need mental health treatment, and some military personnel on active duty have shared that they felt they couldn't obtain mental health treatment as it would be held against them. Our U.S. Congress passed the Clay Hunt Act in memory of a marine veteran who didn't receive the mental health services he needed from the Veteran's Health Administration, and he died by suicide. Suicide prevention in the military is extremely challenging, and I don't propose that I have all the answers. Hopefully, more mental health resources will be provided to our veterans and our current military personnel. It is important that I recognize that the high suicide rate for veterans and current military personnel means that many families of military personnel have been exposed to suicide. Those families definitely need to get counseling support for all members of the family. Suicide is not inherited, it is not fate, it is not destiny, but it can run in families,
largely because of the modeling effect. It is critically important in our families that we tell the truth when a suicide has occurred. In my career, often a student tells me, "I finally figured out what happened to my favorite uncle. He was a marine veteran, and he killed himself eight years ago. Why didn't they tell me the truth then?" My strong recommendation is to always tell the

surviving children, in developmentally appropriate language, the truth about the death by suicide. Then, answer their questions and assure them that help and treatment will be sought for everybody concerned.

You might be wondering, "What is the best help a family can receive when they have lost a loved one to suicide?" I believe strongly that families greatly benefit from participating in suicide survivor groups. I had a parent say to me, "No one could possibly know how badly I hurt after the suicide of my child." My response is that when you go to a suicide survivor group, you're going to be aware that others have gone through, and are coping with, the incredibly complicated grief that you are experiencing. Please, go to one of those meetings and give them a chance to help you. I do want to emphasize that it's important to go to a suicide survivor group because parents have reported when they go to a general survivor group—for example, The Compassionate Friends—and they share that their child died by suicide, a Compassionate Friends member might say, "Oh, my child died of leukemia," and the suicide survivor immediately feels out of place. If you don't know the contacts to obtain information about suicide survivor groups in your region of Montana, contact DPHHS or your local school administration, and they will provide you with that information.

20. How does bullying in elementary school impact suicide in later years?

I addressed a number of issues about bullying in question 18. I do want to emphasize the literature says that we have underestimated the impact of being a bullying victim. Bullying may affect us for decades, so the things that I said about the critical role of schools and parents are very, very important to be able to reduce and eliminate bullying. In addition, it's important to clarify that there is a relationship between bullying and suicide. The research, which is summarized by the Suicide Prevention Resource Center (www.sprc.org) in a brief entitled "Suicide and Bullying," can be summarized with a few statements. There is a strong association between bullying and suicide. The research does not show a causal relationship between bullying and suicide as it is almost impossible to rule out other factors. For example, things like poverty, loss, trauma, mental illness, and abuse. A number of parents believe strongly that bullying caused the suicide of their child and they have actually sued the school district. One of those cases went all the way to the Supreme Court in Kentucky which ruled in favor of the Floyd County School District. It is almost impossible to rule out all the other contributing factors, but it would also be impossible for us to say that being a bullying victim did not contribute to the death by suicide. My strongest hope is that schools have bullying prevention programs and suicide prevention programs and that staff will not hesitate to ask the student known to be a victim of bullying, "Have you thought about giving up? Have you thought your life might be hopeless? Have you thought about dying by suicide?" There is a strong association between bullying and suicide that schools, families, and communities need to recognize.

21. Should schools be using a universal screening tool to help identify students who are at risk?

I believe the best thing to come along in decades to prevent youth suicide is depression screening. I am a strong advocate for SOS Signs of Suicide, which is available at www.mentalhealthscreening.org. Signs of suicide has two major components: The first component is a very well-done video with the motto ACT—Acknowledge, Care, and Tell. The video, available in a middle school version and a high school version, clearly shows young people exhibiting suicidal warning signs. But, their classmates and their teachers identify their warning signs and get them help utilizing ACT. The second component is a brief seven-item questionnaire that contains questions about energy level, joy of life, depression, thoughts of suicide, and suicidal actions. Students at either level in a classroom setting answer the seven questions, turn it over, score it, and immediately know whether they need to see a mental health professional today. SOS is listed in NREPP at SAMHSA. I'm proud to serve on the SOS advisory board, but, speaking honestly, I have found it difficult to convince schools to utilize this universal depression screening. Given the scope of the problem of youth suicide in Montana, I strongly recommend that all middle schools and high schools implement the SOS program as is recommended by Montana DPHHS. I've sometimes been asked, "Well, we've done SOS two years in a row with the same students. Should we do it again?" And I might say, "This year, bring in a mental health speaker talking in classrooms to students, not in an assembly, reviewing suicide prevention and highlight the key components of the motto ACT." I also want to emphasize the SOS program is not expensive, and I believe it is the best program to come along in decades because we are reaching the students themselves, and the Montana DPHHS has funding to provide SOS for schools. Students tell things to each other that they are never going to share with adults. The SOS program teaches students how to respond and stresses getting adult help.

22. **Are affluent communities at a higher risk for suicide?**

I have been involved just in the last two years in responding to suicide contagion and clusters in New Smyrna Beach, FL; Fairfax County, VA; Palo Alto, CA; and Academy School District 20, CO. I believe all of those communities would meet the definition of being affluent. Youth suicide, however, does cross all racial and socio-economic boundaries in our country. The part that is difficult to clearly designate is whether affluence contributed to the suicides in those communities. I might argue that clusters in less affluent communities may have occurred and have stayed under the radar and somehow not been the focus of media stories. The Center for Disease Control, as described in question 1, has been studying suicide contagion in adolescents. They have identified a number of factors, including the following: family reluctant to get mental health services for their children, substance abuse, gun availability, harassment of LGBTQ students, and academic pressure. Those are the factors that we have identified so far. Those epidemiology studies continue, and I believe that the Center for Disease Control will conduct further research. My hope is that school communities and parents who tragically lost their sons and daughters to suicide will contribute to those studies because it can only help us in identifying at-risk youth and preventing further suicides. To summarize, my belief is that affluent communities are at higher risk, but we don't have substantial research to clearly determine if that is the case.

23. **Is there an increased risk of suicide for students with ADHD or sensory issues?**

I am not aware of increased suicide risk for students with sensory issues and hyper-sensitivity. There is growing research that links attention deficit hyperactivity disorder (ADHD) and suicide. Children with ADHD often have coexisting mental health issues, and if their ADHD is untreated, they are especially at risk for frustration, school failure, and depression. Parents are encouraged to obtain the proper treatment for a child identified with ADHD. Personnel such as physicians, psychologists, and school counselors, in addition to parents, are encouraged to monitor these children for signs of depression. Mental health professionals and parents should not be afraid to inquire directly about suicidal thoughts, and if the child discloses suicidal thoughts/actions, then a safety plan needs to be implemented.

24. How can parents best address the "choking game" with their children?

This question has to do with the "choking game," which goes by many different terms, like pass-out, black-out, etc. It's very unfortunate that it is called a game because it can be deadly. Most young people learn about it from another student at school or online. The activity is often engaged in by pairs. One young person might ask the second young person to choke them until they pass out. You must be wondering why they do this, and what the possible benefit is. The "benefit" is that the oxygen to your brain is stopped through the activity and then returns to your brain when the choking has stopped, causing a "high." Students do it to get the "high." The literature discusses that a number of students have gotten the message that drugs are bad—
which is a very important message—but they did not get the message that the choking activity is bad. Some schools have found "good kids"; kids who play on sports teams and kids on student councils actually engaging in this behavior. The activity is particularly dangerous when one young person engages in it in isolation because they pass out and therefore cannot release the pressure from the rope that they have put around their neck. I encourage parents to be alert for the following: Are there ropes and straps in your child's bedroom that simply do not need to be there? Have you noticed your child with bloodshot eyes, coming out of their room disoriented, or having marks on their neck? Have you heard a loud thud like someone falling in their room? The question of how much to discuss this with young people is actually quite challenging. I highly support discussing suicide prevention in a classroom, a small group, or an individual setting. I do not support discussing suicide in an assembly. Likewise, the choking game should not be discussed in an assembly. Additionally, I do not recommend discussing it in a classroom
setting. The reason for this caution is that someone in the classroom will inevitably speak up and say, "Oh, yea. I did it, and I felt really cool. I got the feeling of elation afterwards." This is the problem with discussing it in a group. However, given the tremendous danger of the choking activity, I do believe it is important for the parents of middle school adolescents to have a discussion with them. It might be best brokered with a lead-in question such as "Hey, I heard something about this choking game or activity. What is that?" The parent then listens and talks about the dangers of the behavior. For more information, I encourage everyone to visit Games Adolescents Shouldn't Play, www.gaspinfo.com.

25. What are some effective suicide-prevention programs?

The effective suicide-prevention programs were discussed in question 21. In particular, I highlighted Signs of Suicide (SOS), which is in the NREPP. However, that is not the only program highlighted there. A number of other programs also provide very important prevention information for school staff and parents. I highly recommend that Montana school administrators investigate the NREPP in consultation with OPI, SAM, and DPHHS as they plan training and prevention programs for parents, staff, and, most importantly, students. One of the programs listed there is Sources of Strength, which not only provides a broad approach to teaching young people how to recognize when they or someone they know is suicidal, but also promotes various sources of strength, resiliency, and key skills that promote social and emotional wellness for young people.

26. Should I read my child's texts, Google Hangouts, Facebook, Instagram, etc.? How much should I "snoop"?

This is a great question. I have addressed this in a number of previous questions; refer to the answers to questions 8 and 17. I want to again stress that, as a parent, you know your child the best. You should be in a good position to address whether everything is healthy and appropriate in your child's life right now. If you do not believe that things are healthy and appropriate; if you are concerned about behavior, friendships, and/or websites; and if you are seeing signs of isolation and possibly depression or substance abuse, then it is really important that you snoop. My experience has been that parents are often extremely high on denial, and they are reluctant to acknowledge there is a problem and get help. The first place to start is with the school counselor: "I am concerned about my child for these reasons. Can you give me some information about how things are going at school? Does this seem out of the norm for you? You're trained as a counselor—do I need to get some mental health treatment for my child in the community?" Please, share your concerns with the school counselor and determine whether you need to snoop, and, most importantly, whether you need to seek mental health treatment for your child. To be honest, for the majority of the time in my 36-year career as a psychologist, when the parent described to me what was going on and asked, "Should I be worried? Should I go get help?" the answer was "yes," and the parents knew I was going to say this. They simply needed to hear it. If your child has lost a friend to suicide, I strongly encourage you to monitor their communication to others through social networks.

27. How can schools/parents help students develop coping skills?

Resilience is arguably the biggest word in our vocabulary post 9/11. What is resiliency? Resiliency is learned. The modeling that adults do in our families is very important in order to help our children bounce back from adversity. The keys to resiliency are the following: being comfortable venting and sharing strong emotions, being surrounded by loving and caring family and friends, utilizing problem-solving skills, and always remaining optimistic about the future. These are issues and skills that need to be emphasized starting at the elementary school level through activities and through learning from Americans that have faced incredible misfortune yet persevered. One great example is Abraham Lincoln. He had many misfortunes, lost many elections in a row, before he finally won one. Our school materials should certainly highlight successful people who overcame obstacles in their lives. Parents often wrestle with how much they should share with their children about their own obstacles, difficulties, mistakes, and misfortunes. As a parent, you will be in the best position to determine when to share some of those obstacles and adversities you've experienced. For example, my own children know that I was kicked out of school. I shared with them in the hope that they would not repeat my poor scholarship in the early days of college. None did. I think these are important lessons to share in our families. The most important thing about focusing on resiliency and coping skills is the following: the worth of our children or a student at school should never be in question, nor should our love for them be questioned. This means that we need to be very careful in moments of anger and frustration regarding what exactly we say to them. We should clearly state, "I am disappointed in your misbehavior. However, my love and appreciation for you as a person is never in question. But there will be a consequence." This means that calling a child "stupid" and yelling at them should never take place. Only use statements such as "What can you learn from this? Do you need to apologize? How can you do something to make this right?"

28. At what age should we begin talking to our students about suicide?

It's a challenge to figure out when we should talk to a young person about suicide, both in our homes and in our schools. In our families we need to tell the truth when we have lost a loved one to suicide. Upper elementary school counselors all across this country have emphasized that more and more fifth-graders have expressed suicidal thoughts. However, most adults have never thought we need to talk to nine- and ten-year-olds about suicide. I was involved in a legal case in Blue Springs, MO, where a 10-year-old child drew a picture of himself hanging and wrote, "If someone doesn't stop me, I will hang myself at 4:35 today." He handed that note to a fifth-grade classmate. I'm sorry to tell you that the classmate did not alert an adult because no one had ever talked to her about suicide, and no one had ever anticipated her being in that position. Tragedy was the result. Most NREPP programs are middle school and high school programs. The only program mentioned at the elementary level is the PAX Good Behavior Game, which focuses on appropriate behavior and social skills, not on suicide prevention directly, but it has demonstrated promising results for suicide prevention, and DPHHS has recommended it for every first- or second-grade classroom in Montana. I believe strongly that
we have to get across to elementary students that if something doesn't feel right, if something is giving them a bad headache, or if they have a feeling in the pit of their stomach because something really bad could happen, they need to get adult help. It is my hope that in the next few years, at least for upper elementary, we come out with programs for students that will emphasize that 1-800-SUICIDE (784-2433) and 1-800 272-TALK (8255) are national crisis helplines, which can be called every moment of the day. Additionally, Crisis Text Line is available
24/7 by texting "MT" to 741741. Frankly, the majority of calls to the helpline are not about suicide. They are from kids who are experiencing trauma, bullying, or loss; who don't know where their parents are; who can't find anything to eat in their home; whose electricity has been turned off; or who have had a really bad day at school. So, I'd really like to see the national crisis helpline and the national crisis text line as something that we share with all elementary students. In addition, for students who have an iPhone, if you say to SIRI that you are thinking of killing yourself, the immediate response is to offer to connect you to the national crisis helpline. There is a new program from the state of Washington, a youth-suicide-prevention program for fifth-graders entitled Riding the Waves, which focuses on healthy emotional development and on depression and anxiety. More information is available at
www.yspp.org/curriculum/RidingWaves_curriculum.htm.

29. Will talking to students about suicide/choking game put the ideas in their head?

I've addressed the importance of talking openly and directly with our young children about suicide in several earlier questions. Certainly, do so from the beginning of middle school and through high school. See question 24 where I talk about the importance of speaking with students individually about the dangers of the choking game. I want to reiterate that the reason we have so many suicides is that we do not talk about suicide, and talking about suicide does not plant the idea in someone's head.

30. **How do we respond when our child says, "I'm the worst kid in the world" when they get in trouble or make a bad decision? Is this a warning sign?**

Several previous questions (6, 8, 10, 13, 16, 17, 18, 24, 27, and 28) have talked about the importance of communication between parents and children. What should we say when we have a child who consistently berates themselves, puts themselves down, says things like, "I'm the worst kid in the world. Nobody is as bad as I am"? Obviously, it is very concerning when we have a young person who is making these derogatory statements about themselves. First of all, in our schools and homes, we need to be able to clearly let our children know all of the things we love and appreciate about them. I like to begin every conference about a child by asking the adult present to tell me the things he/she truly loves and appreciates about this child. Frankly, I am the most concerned when a person tells me one thing and then goes to the negative—or when they do not tell me one positive thing at all. I believe that all children do far more right than wrong. Parents need to clearly stress positive qualities for their child. Most importantly, how they love and appreciate the child for who they are. But, what if your child continues these derogatory statements, and they have been pervasive and persistent? Then you need to get mental health treatment for your child. Get them involved in treatment to help build up their self-esteem. Additionally, it is important that all students find their niche. What do I mean by this? Our children need to find an activity where they feel successful. It could be running down the field in football, playing chess, reading books, volunteering in a retirement home, or tutoring a younger child. We simply need to put all children in a position where they are doing something they feel good about. This can go a long way towards alleviating situations in their life that are not going so well. Find an activity that your child can participate in, feel good about, and have a sense of accomplishment about.

31. **How can I help my child who reached out in a positive way to a child who completed suicide?**

This question brings up an important point because many young people in Montana lost someone they knew to suicide. Some of your children may have even reached out and tried to help, yet their friend or classmate still died by suicide. It's important that young people know that we cannot prevent every suicide. The young person who died by suicide traveled a very long road. It was never one thing, it was never one person—nothing and no one is to blame. I have often shared with young people devastated by the suicide of their friend that they didn't really know much about suicide. They didn't think it could happen to someone they knew and cared about. Unfortunately, no one had ever prepared them by providing information about suicide and what to do to intervene with their friend. I know because I lost my own father to suicide, and I missed the obvious warning signs he was exhibiting. I will forever second-guess myself for failing to take action to get him mental health treatment. I have found some comfort in getting involved in suicide prevention, and I believe that many survivors of suicide ultimately reach a point where they also get involved in suicide prevention because they just may be able to save the life of someone else's loved one. I would say to these young people who lost a friend to suicide that, in many ways, this will be something you will always feel sad about, but it's very important that you give yourself permission to go on with your life and focus on what is in front of you, so you can be successful. There will be times when this will be especially difficult for you. This would logically be the birthday that the deceased would have had or the anniversary of his or her death. Do not hesitate to reach out to your parents and counselors at that time. As months and years go by, it will get a little easier, but it is always something that will stay with you. Many people who have lost loved ones to suicide decide ultimately that they would like to get into a helping profession as a counselor, physician, or social worker, for example. The adults who are reading this question should always be there for the child who has lost a friend to suicide. I've been aware that young people have often been told by well-meaning adults, "Oh, you should be over that by now. You shouldn't be focusing on that. I'm tired of hearing you talk about the friend(s) you've lost to suicide." Obviously, these are not the correct responses from adults. Instead, the answer should be "I'm always here to listen to you. Please, know there will be a lot of ups and downs, and I'm here for you every step of the way. Things will get better, and if you feel they are not getting better, then we are going to get you professional help." I would strongly recommend that many young people in Montana do, in fact, need private mental

health counseling as a result of losing friends to suicide. Please, contact the school counseling office and get a referral to recommended providers in your community that are skilled in working with teenagers with trauma and loss issues.

32. **Are there times when well-intentioned peer/teacher support exacerbates normal teenage angst? What are the limits on this support, if any?**

This question has to do with issue of support for young people that have experienced trauma or loss and with young people who are depressed. Please read my answer to question 31, which simply states that our schools and families often underestimate the effects of trauma, loss, and, especially, suicide on our children and students. I don't believe that too much support can be offered. We need support in school, support in our home, support in local mental health agencies, and support in our local churches. We need to continue to revisit the losses and suicides with our affected young people and not hesitate to ask how they are doing. They will quickly let us know if they are doing okay, and they will probably thank you for asking. As we look ahead, students are going to be aware of the anniversary of their friends' deaths, and they will be aware of the birthdays the deceased would have had and the graduation ceremony they will not attend. I'm not recommending that the school should make a PA announcement about the loss of the student a year ago. No. I'm simply talking about parents being aware of that anniversary. Teachers and counselors should also be aware of that anniversary and simply sit down with students and say, "I know that tomorrow is the day a year ago that your friend died by suicide. That might be on your mind. I'm here to listen if you'd like to talk about it." I simply do not believe there can be too much support after the suicide of students. One Canadian study clarified that we underestimate the impact of a suicide and focus on too few people being at risk. The same study said that losing a student to suicide might affect classmates and schools for as long as six years. I know that is something that people reading the answer to this question do not want to hear, but it certainly emphasizes the points I've made about Montana schools who have lost students to suicide being in this for the long haul. It's necessary to provide support for affected students now and for many years to come.

Appendix 2: After a Suicide: Challenging Time for Schools

After a Suicide: Postvention for Schools

Answering Student Questions and Providing Support

Scott Poland, Co-Director of the Suicide and Violence Prevention Office

Nova Southeastern University in Fort Lauderdale, FL

Richard Lieberman, Loyola Marymount University

The authors can be contacted at spoland@nova.edu and richard.lieberman@lmu.edu

Overview

The aftermath of a youth suicide is a sad and challenging time for a school. Postvention is a term coined by Shneidman to describe helpful and appropriate acts after a dire event. The term has become synonymous with the challenging aftermath of suicide, and few events are scarier for a school and community than the suicide of a young person. The major tasks for suicide postvention are to help your students and fellow faculty to manage the understandable feelings of shock, grief, and confusion. The major focus should be grief resolution and prevention of further suicides.

The research literature estimates that once a suicide happens, the chances of another death by suicide increases dramatically. The following suggestions are intended to guide staff during this difficult time:

- It is important to be honest with students about the scope of the problem of youth suicide and the key role that everyone (including the students) plays in **prevention**.
- It is important to balance being truthful and honest without violating the privacy of the suicide victim and his/her family and to take great care not to glorify their actions.
- It is important to have the facts of the incident, to be alert to speculation and erroneous information that may be circulating, and to assertively, yet kindly, redirect students toward productive, healthy conversation.
- Center for Disease Control research has found that the teenagers most susceptible to suicide contagion are those believed to be: students who backed out of a suicide pact, students who had a very negative last interaction with the victim, students who now realize they missed warning signs, and students with their own set of childhood adversities/previous suicidal behavior who need not have known the victim.
- Potentially high-risk groups include white, Hispanic, Alaska Native, American Indian, African-American, and Asian-American youth.
- LGBTQ students can be at additional risk, particularly if they have experienced parental rejection or gender-based bullying. Utilize your campus Gay–Straight Alliance.
- It is important that students not feel that the suicide victim has been erased, and that students be provided an opportunity to talk about the deceased.
- Numerous professional associations caution that memorials not be dramatic or permanent and, instead, encourage activities that focus on living memorials, such as funding suicide prevention.
- Suicide is always on the minds of numerous high school students, and the national YRBSS survey for 2015 found 17.7% of students seriously considered suicide, and 8.6% reported making a suicide attempt in the last year.

- School personnel are encouraged to monitor social media after a suicide occurs as vulnerable youths often connect with each other online. Learn about safe messaging.
- School personnel often consider postponing previously scheduled suicide-prevention programs if a suicide has occurred, but prevention information is needed more than ever as suicide postvention focuses on prevention of further suicides.
- It is essential that school personnel are trained to recognize signs of distress, including depression, anxiety, substance abuse, and thoughts of suicide, so they can approach students to discuss their concerns. Kognito's At-Risk for High School Educators is an interactive gatekeeper program that uses role-play with animated and responsive avatars. Participants engage in a simulated conversation with the help of a virtual coach. The program is listed as evidence-based on the Suicide Prevention Resource Center website (www.sprc.org). More information about Kognito programs is available at www.kognito.com.
- Schools are often reluctant to implement depression-screening programs that are available for middle school and high school students. Depression screening reaches students themselves, helps them to identify symptoms of depression, and encourages them to seek adult help for themselves or a friend. The SOS Signs of Suicide program includes empowering videos where students learn how to help themselves or their friends through ACT (Acknowledge, Care, and Treatment). SOS is listed as evidence-based on the Suicide Prevention Resource Center website (www.sprc.org). Detailed information about SOS can be found at www.mentalhealthscreening.org.
- National research has found that talking with youth about suicide does not cause them to think of it and, in fact, provides the opportunity for them to relieve anxiety and unburden themselves. The Jason Flatt Act, which focuses on mandated training annually for school staff on suicide prevention, has been passed in 30% of all states. More information about the Jason Foundation is available at www.jasonfoundation.com.
- Major protective factors identified by the World Health Organization are the following: stable families, positive connections at school, good connections with other youth, religious involvement, lack of access to lethal weapons, access to mental health care, and awareness of crisis hotline resources.

Commonly Asked Questions and Appropriate Responses:

Why did he /she die by suicide?

We are never going to know the answer to that question as the answer has died with him/her. The focus needs to be on helping students with their thoughts and feelings and on everyone in the school community working together to prevent future suicides.

What method did they use to end their life?

Answer specifically with information as to the method, such as he/she shot herself or died by hanging, but do not go into explicit details such as what was the type of gun or rope used, the condition of the body, etc.

Why didn't God stop him/her?

There are varying religious beliefs about suicide, and you are all free to have your own beliefs. However, many religious leaders have used the expression "God sounded the alarm but could not stop him/her.

God has embraced them, yes, and he/she is in whatever afterlife you believe in, but God is actually saddened that he/she did not stay on this earth and do God's work over their natural lifetime."

What should I say about him/her, now that they have made the choice to die by suicide?

It is important that we remember the positive things about them and respect their privacy and that of their family. Please be sensitive to the needs of their close friends and family members.

Didn't he/she make a poor choice, and is it okay to be angry with them?

They did make a very poor choice, and research has found that many young people who survived a suicide attempt are very glad to be alive and never attempted suicide again. You have permission for any and all your feelings in the aftermath of suicide, and it is okay to be angry with them.

The suicide of a young person has been compared to throwing a rock into a pond spreading ripple effects through the school, church, and the community, and there is often a search for a simple explanation. These ripple effects have never been greater with the existence of social networks (e.g., Facebook). It is recommended that school staff and parents monitor what is being posted on social networks in the aftermath of a suicide. Suicide is a multifaceted event, and sociological, psychological, biological, and physiological elements were all present to some degree. The suicide is no one's fault; yet, it is everyone's fault, and suicide prevention is everyone's responsibility. Many individuals who died by suicide had untreated mental illnesses, most likely depression, and it is important that everyone is aware of resources that are available in their school and community, so that needed treatment can be obtained. It is always important that everyone knows the warning signs of suicide, and they are outlined in great detail on websites referenced in this handout.

Isn't someone or something to blame for this suicide?

The suicide victim made a very poor choice, and there is no one to blame. The decision to die by suicide involved every interaction and experience throughout the young person's entire life up until the moment they died; yet, it did not have to happen. It is the fault of no one. No one person, no one thing, is ever to blame.

How can I cope with this suicide?

It is important to remember what or who has helped you cope when you have had to deal with sad things in your life before. Please turn to the important adults in your life for help and share your feelings with them. It is important to maintain normal routines and proper sleeping and eating habits and to engage in regular exercise. Please avoid drugs and alcohol. Resiliency, which is the ability to bounce back from adversity, is a learned behavior. Everyone does the best when surrounded by friends and family who care about us and by viewing the future in a positive manner.

What is an appropriate memorial to a suicide victim?

The most appropriate memorial is a living one such as a scholarship fund or contributions to support suicide prevention. The American Foundation for Suicide Prevention (www.afsp.org) and the Suicide Prevention Resource Center (www.sprc.org) published in 2011 an excellent guide for postvention entitled *After a Suicide: A Toolkit for Schools*, which is available on either websites. The guide provides specific guidelines to balance the often-felt needs that students have to do something after a suicide without glorifying the suicide victim, which might contribute to other teenagers considering suicide.

How serious is the problem of youth suicide?

In 2015, suicide was the second leading cause of death for teenagers, and the tenth leading cause of death for all Americans. More than 44,000 Americans, including approximately 4,500 youths, die by suicide annually, and suicide rates have increased for Americans in general but most notably for middle- school-age girls. Many young people think about suicide. The national Youth Risk Behavior Survey (YRBS) for 2015 found 17.7% of high school students reported seriously considering suicide, and 8.6% of high school students actually made a suicide attempt in the last year. These figures represent increases from the 2013 YRBS survey. Ninth-grade students are the most at risk. National research has found that talking with youth about suicide does not cause them to think of it and in fact provides the opportunity for them to relieve anxiety and unburden themselves.

What are the warning signs of suicide?

The most common signs are the following: making a suicide attempt, verbal and written statements about death and suicide, fascination and preoccupation with death, giving away of prized possessions, saying goodbye to friends and family, making out wills, and dramatic changes in behavior and personality.

What should I do if I believe someone to be suicidal?

Listen to them, support them and let them know that they are not the first person to feel this way. There is help available, and mental health professionals such as counselors and psychologists have special training to help young people who are suicidal. Do not keep suicidal behavior a secret—save a life by getting adult help as that is what a good friend does, and someday your friend will thank you.

How does the crisis hotline work?

We are very fortunate to have nationally certified crisis hotlines in many cities that are available 24 hours a day and manned by trained volunteers. There is also a 24-hour national suicide hotline, which can be reached via **1-800-SUICIDE (784-2433) or 1-800-273-TALK (8255)**. In addition, many young people today are utilizing the Crisis Text Line, www.crisistextline.org.

How can I make a difference in suicide prevention?

Know the warnings signs, listen to your friends carefully, do not hesitate to get adult help, remember that most youth suicides can be prevented, and become aware of ways to get involved with suicide prevention. High school students can volunteer in some cities and be trained to answer the teen line. Please, contact the local crisis hotline for more information. One person can make the difference and prevent a suicide.

Where can I go for more information about preventing suicide?

The American Association of Suicidology (AAS): www.suicidology.org

The Jason Foundation: www.jasonfoundation.com

Yellow Ribbon Suicide Prevention Program: www.yellowribbon.org

The American Foundation for Suicide Prevention: www.afsp.org The

Suicide Prevention Resource Center at www.sprc.org

Nova Southeastern University: www.nova.edu/suicideprevention. Our three training videos focus on suicide awareness, suicide assessment, and suicide postvention in schools.

How well do families who lost a child to suicide cope with the loss?

The literature well documents the devastating effect of suicide on the family, and that family members often feel isolated. Research studies conducted 15 months after the suicide indicate that the families have resumed normal functioning; however, they are profoundly affected, especially when there is little explanation for the suicide of their loved one. Family members may experience anger towards those they believe are somehow responsible, loss of interest in their employment or school work, increased absences, disrupted sleeping and eating patterns, grief, helplessness, abandonment, isolation, loneliness, shame, and guilt. Suicide survivors have more difficulty with the grieving process than survivors of losses from other causes than suicide. Survivors often reported feeling uncomfortable with the naturally occurring support systems, and school and community members are often unsure of what to say and how to reach out to those who lost a family member to suicide.

If a family member has a preexisting mental health condition, it will likely be exacerbated, and substance abuse will increase. Families reported receiving less support than they deemed necessary, and what support they did receive was often poorly timed and especially ineffective for younger siblings. Research studies have also found that approximately 50% of the time children were not told the truth that the cause of death was suicide. Children often find out the truth at a later date and are upset that they were not told the truth. Bereavement was complicated when family members had deeply religious beliefs and moral convictions against suicide. Family physicians and school personnel who are knowledgeable about helping survivors cope and available community resources can play a significant role in supporting the grieving family. Family members often receive comfort and find meaning in becoming involved in suicide prevention.

Scott Poland, EdD, NCSP, is the Co-Director of the Suicide and Violence Prevention Office at Nova Southeastern University (www.nova.edu/suicideprevention) and has over 35 years of school experience. He was previously the Prevention Division Director for AAS, has worked in the aftermath of many youth suicides, and has led numerous teams following suicide clusters. He is the author of five books and numerous chapters and articles on the subjects of youth suicide and school crisis. He is the coauthor of a 2015 book entitled *Suicide in Schools*, published by Routledge. He has also provided U.S. Congressional testimony on several occasions, focused on school violence and youth suicide prevention.

Richard Lieberman, MA, NCSP, is currently Lead Consultant for the CalMHSA Student Mental Health Initiative for the Los Angeles County Office of Education. He is a lecturer in the School of Education at Loyola Marymount University, and from 1986 to 2011 he coordinated Suicide Prevention Services for Los Angeles Unified School District. Mr. Lieberman is coauthor of *School Crisis Prevention and Intervention: The PREPaRE Model* and *Best Practices in Suicide Intervention (IV, V, & VI)* for the National Association of School Psychologists. He has written numerous book chapters and articles on youth suicide prevention, crisis intervention, and responding to self-injurious students in the schools, and he has appeared in many videos, including the HBO documentary "Suicide." Mr. Lieberman serves on the steering committee for the national Suicide Prevention Resource Center and two task forces of the National Action Alliance for Suicide Prevention

Appendix 3: Suicide Risk Factors for Montana Youth

A youth suicide is almost always the result of an untreated or undertreated mental illness. Thus, there is an urgency for prevention—especially because new statistics from the Centers for Disease Control and Prevention (CDC) reveal that suicides in the United States are at a near 30-year high. In fact, according to the CDC, suicide is the second leading cause of death for youths between the ages of 10 and 24, resulting in more than 5,000 lives lost each year. Embedded in those numbers is an alarming rise in suicide deaths among girls ages 10 to 14.

> A challenge for suicide prevention in schools is the incorrect belief that we should not ask a student directly about suicidal thoughts as then they might start thinking about suicide. Nothing could be further from the truth! Having the opportunity to talk about their suicidal thoughts provides the student the opportunity to unburden him- or herself and to receive the needed support and treatment.

Suicide is preventable, and evidence-based mental health treatments exist. A challenge for suicide prevention in homes and communities is the belief that if guns were locked up, a suicidal individual would just find another way to die by suicide. Extensive research has documented that removing lethal means from a suicidal individual through safe gun storage drastically reduces the risk of suicide. Research on this issue and suggestions for discussions on safe gun storage are available at www.hsph.harvard.edu/means-matter/.

It is important to note that serious mental health issues often reveal themselves during adolescence and emerging adulthood. The National Alliance on Mental Illness states that such conditions are common among teens and young adults, affecting 1 in 5 with half exhibiting signs by age 14 and three-quarters by age 24. Additionally, estimates are that approximately 20% of all adolescents suffer from depression during the tumultuous teenage years, but that only about 20% of them ever receive any mental health treatment. One of the greatest challenges for youth suicide prevention in Montana is to teach young people how to respond to help a friend who is suicidal, to know the importance of involving a trusted adult, and to understand that suicides can be prevented and are not fate or destiny. The Jason Foundation (www.jasonfoundation.com) has a free app called A Friend Asks, which Montana students are encouraged to download to their phones. The app provides guidance on what to do if a friend is suicidal.

Made in the USA
Middletown, DE
20 January 2022

59084850R10086